PRAY
A to Z

PRAY
A to Z

A Practical Guide to Pray
for Your Community

AMELIA RHODES

WORTHY™
Inspired

Published by Worthy Inspired, an imprint of Worthy Publishing Group, a division of Worthy Media, Inc., One Franklin Park, 6100 Tower Circle, Suite 210, Franklin, TN 37067.

WORTHY is a registered trademark of Worthy Media, Inc.

HELPING PEOPLE EXPERIENCE THE HEART OF GOD

Library of Congress Control Number: 2016950778

ISBN: 978-1-61795-745-1

For foreign and subsidiary rights, contact rights@worthypublishing.com

Cover Design: Melissa Reagan
Cover Image: Shutterstock.com

Printed in the United States of America

16 17 18 19 20 21 LBM 10 9 8 7 6 5 4 3 2 1

For Kedron.
Without you, this project would still be
on 3 x 5 cards scribbled in pencil on my desk.
Thank you for your constant belief in me and this project.
I love spending my life with you.

For Ilana and Titus.
You light my life with joy
and are two of God's greatest gifts to me.
I'm honored to be your mama.

Contents

Introduction

I jolted awake at 2:00 a.m. this morning to a shrill, heart-stopping alarm blasting from my cell phone. I nearly fell out of bed onto my head while scrambling to find the phone somewhere on the floor. I grabbed the screaming phone and fumbled for a button—any button—to turn off the dreadful sound before reading an Amber Alert for two missing children from a nearby community. I scanned the grim details about the alleged abductor, and my heart moaned in lament.

I crawled back into bed willing my heart rate to slow, and stared into the darkness above my head. My racing thoughts turned to prayers. "Lord, please watch over these two children. Wherever they are, whatever they're experiencing, be their Guard. This moment changes their lives forever. Help them know Your presence today and for the rest of their lives. Please guide the police as they search."

My heart constricted as though the snake of darkness might squeeze the life right out of me. So much hurt. So much pain. "Why, God? Why does it seem we only hurt each other?"

Five hours later as I groggily began my day, I checked the news for an update. A policeman had found the children 1,100 miles away, and they were being held in safe custody. I sobbed as I read more details of the story and realized what those precious children had experienced during the night. I put a little extra "oomph" into my morning kiss good-bye with my two children.

Midday, I scrolled my Facebook feed to see if I was the

only one jarred awake at 2:00 a.m. Some friends grumbled about the rude awakening. Most, however, described how they, too, spent that wee hour of the morning praying for the children and their safe return home.

A community praying for children they didn't even know. What a beautiful picture of the body of Christ.

"See?" God's Spirit whispered. "There is still light in this world. Remember, I am the light, and My light still shines in so many. You do more than just hurt each other. You are also capable of great love for each other."

If only an audible alarm could jolt us out of our spiritual slumber every day and call us into prayerful action for our community.

How would our communities change if we didn't just say, "I'll pray for you," but we actually did pray—deeply, intensely, and purposefully?

Even when the news doesn't wake me early in the morning with an urgent alarm, great needs press in around me every day.

A year and a half ago I sat on my bedroom floor Spirit-groaning like Paul describes in Romans 8:26: "In the same way, the Spirit helps us in our weakness. We do not know what we ought to pray for, but the Spirit himself intercedes for us through wordless groans."

That day, a friend had called to say her father had been diagnosed with cancer. Another friend had sent an e-mail with a discouraging update about his family's already years-long adoption process. A third friend had texted with news that his wife was leaving him for another man.

Each message closed with, "Will you please pray?"

"Of course. Absolutely," I replied to each one.

Yet I felt so inadequate. Prayer has never been one of my strong disciplines. I often prayed for people on the spot, for fear I would forget later. I certainly didn't want to lie about praying.

That day, during my Spirit-groanings for these dear friends, I also asked for help with my prayer discipline.

"There has to be a better way. I want to remember. I want to be a participant, not just a bystander."

As I rose to finish my day, a thought came to me—a thought that would forever change the way I pray.

A is for adoption. I counted several friends who were waiting for adoptions to be complete, and others who had recently brought their adoptive children home.

B is for bullying. I remembered my teacher friends and the students in my kids' classes who've suffered from bullying behavior.

C is for cancer. I listed at least a dozen people I knew who were battling cancer.

D is for depression. I remembered all the family members and friends I knew who were struggling through depression and anxiety on a daily basis.

What if, instead of having one long prayer list, I prayed for people by topic, through the entire alphabet?

I grabbed a sheet of paper and within an hour had topics for nearly the entire alphabet. The next day, I met my friends Cindy and Carrie for coffee and quietly mentioned how I was going to start praying A to Z through the needs of the community. I showed them my list, and their eyes lit up.

"Will you share it with me? That's something I would use, too."

"Me, too, please. I often feel overwhelmed and just don't know where to start or how to remember to pray for everyone."

I wasn't alone in feeling like an inadequate pray-er.

That's when I realized God is raising the alarm. He is calling His people to prayer. As the world grows darker, His light shines brighter.

As I prayed from A to Z, I no longer felt overwhelmed. In fact, I found myself praying for more people and more struggles than ever before. I experienced a peace and a lightness in prayer that I hadn't known in a long time.

As the idea spread among my friends, I began to hear stories. My friend Erin picked up the idea and started praying A to Z with her kids. She told me they prayed for a family who had been waiting years to adopt a child. The morning after praying through "A for Adoption," she woke to an e-mail from her friends saying a child had been placed with them. Erin woke her children with the incredible news. What a joy to pray with her kids and see God's answer so soon!

My mom told me she had never noticed how difficult it was for families in her church with special needs children to enjoy an entire worship service. She started to see how often they were called out of the service. She told me, "Now that I'm praying A to Z, God is revealing to me people's needs that I hadn't seen before."

As we pray for our communities' deepest needs, we bring His light into the darkest corners.

No problem is too great for our Father to handle. In fact, as I began to also praise God from A to Z, I realized how every need is fulfilled in who He is.

From A to Z, I hope you'll join me in praying for the specific needs of your community and begin to experience the lightness of joy, peace, and hope that comes from the Father.

How to Use This Book

The book is divided by letter with five topics per letter. The first three topics for each letter are prayers of petition asking God to work in a certain area of your life or the lives of others in your community. The last two topics for each letter are prayers of praise acknowledging who God is and where you've seen His work.

Don't ignore the prayers of praise; they're important. When you start to focus on all the needs around you, your heart gets overwhelmed quickly. The darkness is palpable, and the needs can seem impossible. Yet, when you take time to praise God for who He is, you will begin to see how every need you have is met in Him. You'll pray for those struggling with bullying, bulimia and eating disorders, and bankruptcy; and then you'll praise God that He is the Bread of Life and your Burden Bearer. Just recognizing who He is lightens the load because you've placed the heaviness where it belongs—on His strong shoulders.

Each topic includes a verse and a few prompts to get you started. The written-out prayers are meant to be a springboard for your own conversations with God. My prayer is that through those few sentences, the Holy Spirit will bring to mind situations in your life and community and move you into deeper prayer.

Personal Use

God's love and care for you and your community is personal.

Use this book as a guide and personalize it. Write in the margins. List people, organizations, and situations specific to your community. Update it as you see God move. Write down your praises. Mark it up as a record of how God is working. I've found this helps me pay attention and be alert to God's movement.

How you use this book will be as unique as you are.

Maybe you'll carry it in a purse or computer bag and spend extra minutes waiting for appointments or sitting in the car line at school to pray through one topic.

Maybe you'll keep it by your bedside and pray through one letter each night, going through the alphabet once a month.

Maybe you'll keep it on the kitchen counter or your desk and check in with God throughout the day.

The options are endless. I'm finding prayer can happen everywhere, not just on my knees by the bed or during a few minutes of quiet at church. I'm learning to direct my internal conversations back to God all day long.

Group Use

This is a book about praying for your community, and what better way to do so than actually praying *with* your community?

Whether it's your family gathered around the table for a meal together a few times a week, a small group of friends who meet for coffee once a month, or a church group that meets on a regular basis, you can use this guide to direct your prayers together.

Maybe you pray through one letter each time you gather, with each person in the group praying out loud for one topic. Maybe each person takes a whole letter. Maybe you walk around your neighborhood as a group and pray through a letter each time.

However you choose to use the guide, allow God's Spirit to draw you closer to each other and Himself as you pray through your community's most challenging situations and give praise for His mighty work.

What This Book Is Not

This is not a book on how to pray. Other authors have written helpful books on the mechanics and meaning of prayer. A couple of my favorites include: *Prayer: Experiencing Awe and Intimacy with God* by Timothy Keller (Viking, 2014) and *Too Busy Not to Pray: Slowing Down to Be with God* by Bill Hybels (IVP Books, 2008). Both of these men taught me through their books how to go deeper in my prayer life, listen to God's Spirit, and incorporate Scripture into praying.

This book also isn't a set of written-out prayers for you to mindlessly read. Rather, see this as a conversation starter, an icebreaker, to prompt your conversations with God. It's in no way meant to be a formula to recite, but a guide to begin a deeper communication with your heavenly Father.

Keep in mind that prayer is a conversation, meaning it's two-way. Speak and listen. Listen for God's Spirit to prompt you with thoughts and Scripture. As you listen, you'll find your conversations with God changing. Hybels's book *Too Busy Not to Pray* has great thoughts on how to listen for the Spirit's voice.

However you use this book, my prayer is that you and your community will be transformed by a deepening love for the Father and experience the peace that comes from laying your burdens at His feet.

Adoption

But those who hope in the LORD will renew their strength.
They will soar on wings like eagles; they will run
and not grow weary, they will walk and not be faint.

ISAIAH 40:31

Pray for waiting adoptive families, waiting children, host families, orphanages, and adoption agencies. Remember to include families who have adopted in years past and pray for any struggles just now surfacing with their children.

Father, I pray for every child to be part of a loving family. Be with these families and provide for their financial, emotional, and physical needs as they adopt. Give wisdom to the adoption agencies and host families. Comfort birth parents as they make the hard choice to release their child. Watch over children as they wait for their forever family. I pray all will feel Your loving arms around them as they transition to a new reality. Continue to knit together these families who have completed their adoptions. May a supportive and loving community surround them through all the struggles of parenthood. When challenges come, when hurtful words are said, when fear and uncertainty creep in, I pray You will remain in the middle. Amen.

Abuse

My comfort in my suffering is this:
Your promise preserves my life.

PSALM 119:50

Pray for those suffering from physical, verbal, emotional, and sexual abuse, for their safety and the ability to seek and receive help. Pray that those with abusive behavior would be convicted and reached with Christ's love. Pray for organizations that provide safety and counsel for those suffering from abuse of any kind.

Father, I lift up all who live under the heavy weight of abuse. Many in my community suffer in silence every day. Provide courage to speak up and grant safety as they seek help. Give me eyes to see their hurt and wisdom to know how to offer love in helpful ways. Provide for the organizations in my community that offer counseling and safe places of respite. I pray those with abusive behavior will be convicted, humbled, and experience the transforming power of Your Spirit in their lives. May all involved come to know the truth of who You are and how You love them no matter what they have done or what has happened to them. You are the great Healer of wounded hearts and minds, and I ask for Your healing power. Amen.

Alcoholism

Do not get drunk on wine, which leads to debauchery.
Instead, be filled with the Spirit.

EPHESIANS 5:18

Pray for individuals struggling with alcoholism, for their families and friends, and for the organizations in your community that offer support for recovery.

Father, I bring before You those struggling with alcoholism. Alcoholism is a thief that destroys joy, peace, families, and marriages. Provide strength and comfort to their families, and the courage to speak to their loved one about seeking help. Give peace about hard decisions they need to make for their family's safety. Protect young children in the home. Help the ones struggling with dependence on alcohol to realize the damage it is causing to their physical and mental health. Help them realize alcohol cannot fill whatever hole they feel in their lives. Instead, may they see the power that comes from being filled with Your Spirit. Provide peace, endurance, and hope for all involved. Provide for the organizations and churches in the community who offer counseling, support groups, and rehabilitation. Show me how to speak truth in love when needed and how to offer Your love. Amen.

Abundance

*Grace and peace be yours in abundance through the knowledge
of God and of Jesus our Lord. His divine power has given us
everything we need for a godly life through our knowledge
of him who called us by his own glory and goodness.*

2 PETER 1:2–3

Take time to praise God for His abundance for your physical
needs and for how He has met your spiritual needs through
Jesus Christ. Thank God for abundantly meeting the needs of
which you aren't yet aware.

Father, You are a God of abundance. The same abundant
power and creativity that filled the vast heavens with stars and
layered beauty in the Grand Canyon is also inside me. Thank
You for the knowledge You have given me of Yourself. You
lack nothing. I give praise for how You have shared Your abundance with me through Your divine power and have given me
everything I need to live a godly life through Jesus Christ.
Thank You for the abundance of grace and peace and other
abundant gifts in my life. Whatever I face today—whatever
heartache or struggle comes my way, or when I feel inadequate
to meet the task—I offer praise, for You have already supplied
all I need through Your great and abundant power. I place my
trust in Your abundance today. Amen.

Almighty

Who is he, this King of glory?
The LORD Almighty—he is the King of glory.

PSALM 24:10

Take time to praise God as the Almighty—for His might and power over sin, darkness, and every struggle you face. Offer praise that His strength is incomparable and is available to you.

Father, You are the God Almighty. You are the Lord of hosts, the King of glory, and the all-powerful Lord of the heavenly army. No one can match Your power and might. No power of darkness or evil can defeat You. No situation I face today or tomorrow is too great for You. Thank You for making Your strength available to me through Your Holy Spirit. I look forward to the day when You will show Your power to all, and every knee will bow and every tongue confess that You are Lord (Romans 14:11). Today, I bend my knee and submit my life to You, King of my life and my Lord Almighty. I believe You are who You say You are. May all who see my life see You and Your almighty power shining through me. Amen.

Bullying

Have I not commanded you? Be strong and courageous.
Do not be afraid; do not be discouraged,
for the LORD your God will be with you wherever you go.

JOSHUA 1:9

———————————

Pray for children who live in the fear and torment caused by bullying behavior. Pray for teachers and parents to find solutions, and for the hearts of children with intimidating and mean behavior to be changed.

———————————

Father, devastating stories resulting from bullying behavior often fill the news and bring such heartbreak. I ask for Your courage and strength for teachers, counselors, parents, and students as they confront this behavior. Provide wisdom as they support and care for the targeted children. May those who live in the fear and shadow of bullying behavior know the presence of Your love, and know You are with them wherever they go. Help them experience Your protection and see how valuable their lives are. Equip them to speak up against the aggression by the power of Your Spirit. Enable them to reach out to trusted adults and give those adults wisdom to act on their behalf. I pray You would change the hearts of those with aggressive behavior. Give them compassion. Heal their hurts and redeem their stories. Heal our communities, and teach us how to love even the most difficult people with Your love. Amen.

Bulimia and Eating Disorders

Surely God is my help;
the Lord is the one who sustains me.

PSALM 54:4

Pray for men and women of all ages who struggle with bulimia, anorexia, and other eating disorders. Pray for people to surround them with God's love and for the counselors who assist them.

Father, food is a beautiful gift from You—not just to feed and sustain our bodies, but also for our enjoyment. I bring _____ to You and ask that they would understand how valuable they are to You and to the people who surround them. Help all accept themselves as You've created them. Heal their innermost beings. May they be engaged with a community that will speak truth and love into their lives. Enable them to turn to You for comfort and meaning, not to food or a number on a scale. Help them surrender control to You, and enable them to see Your care and gentleness toward them. Give wisdom, patience, and understanding to the parents, friends, coworkers, and counselors who walk this journey with them. May each person experience Your healing presence. Amen.

Bankruptcy

*Therefore I tell you, do not worry about your life, what you will
eat or drink; or about your body, what you will wear.
Is not life more than food, and the body more than clothes?
Look at the birds of the air; they do not sow or reap or store away
in barns, and yet your heavenly Father feeds them.
Are you not much more valuable than they?*

MATTHEW 6:25–26

Pray for those who face bankruptcy, for their physical needs
to be met, for worry and fear to be alleviated, and for wisdom
to know how to move forward.

Father, I ask for Your peace and wisdom for those facing bankruptcy and serious financial trouble. Whatever the situation
may be, whatever their fears, anxieties, and needs for tomorrow, may they experience a peace and calm that can come only
from You. As they work through the legal paperwork, and all
that entails, give them clarity and focus to complete the task.
Provide sound counsel in the form of trustworthy lawyers
and financial mentors. As they rebuild for the future, please
remove any shame or guilt they may feel, and surround them
with a supportive and generous community that will help
them rebuild their finances. Amen.

Bread of Life

Then Jesus declared, "I am the bread of life.
Whoever comes to me will never go hungry,
and whoever believes in me will never be thirsty."

JOHN 6:35

Praise God for His provision through Jesus as the Bread of Life. Recognize how He is your spiritual sustenance and satisfies your hunger and thirst for meaning and belonging. Thank Him for supplying all of your needs.

God, You are the Bread of Life. I've often sought many things to fill my hunger and thirst for value and meaning. Possessions, wealth, food, drink, relationships, and power do not fill the ache in my soul. You alone satisfy my cravings for purpose. You quench my thirst for meaning and belonging. Today, rather than seeking meaningless things to fill my life, I seek a grateful heart for Your sustenance. In You I find all I need for my daily life. You've given me a place at Your banquet table, and I feast on the good fruit You have given—love, joy, peace, patience, kindness, goodness, faithfulness, gentleness, and self-control. I praise You for this grace and for Your sustaining work in my life every day. Thank You for supplying all of my needs. Amen.

Burden Bearer

Praise be to the Lord, to God our Savior,
who daily bears our burdens.
PSALM 68:19

Praise God for how He bears your burdens each day. Take time to list what He has helped you carry, and give thanks for how you've seen His help. Praise Him for carrying your burdens in the past and recognize He is able to carry today's burdens and the unknown burdens of the future.

God, I echo the Psalmist's words: "Praise be to the Lord, to God [my] Savior, who daily bears [my] burdens." I give praise for how You've helped me with these heavy burdens. Your hand has been present in guiding, helping, and caring for me. Even when I could not see Your hand, You were still present, helping in ways I may not have noticed. I cast my cares upon You, and give praise for Your faithfulness to carry each one. When I attempt to handle them on my own and struggle under the weight, remind me that You are the faithful Bearer of my burdens. When I wake up overwhelmed by what the day holds, remind me that You are the Great I AM and will carry me through today. There is no one greater and more able than You. Thank You for bearing my burdens. Amen.

Cancer

The human spirit can endure in sickness,
but a crushed spirit who can bear?

PROVERBS 18:14

Pray for those who suffer from cancer, and pray for their families, for the doctors and nurses caring for them, and for researchers to find effective treatments and cures. Pray for encouragement and healing, for God's honor and glory.

Father, I bring the families to You who are battling cancer. I ask for Your healing for the patient and for Your sustaining strength for their caregivers. Calm their minds, alleviate their fears, and enable them to rest well today. Bring a renewed sense of hope and peace. Protect them from depression, and bring a good word of encouragement when they need it most. May the oncology staff have an endless supply of compassion, courage, and patience. Give wisdom as they make challenging decisions, especially in crisis moments. Please be with siblings or children who are feeling isolation and disruption of their routine. Provide a community to physically, spiritually, and emotionally surround the family with Your love and practical help. Provide researchers with a greater understanding of the body and this disease so they may continue to develop effective treatments and cures. May all know that You are the God of comfort, a God who is with us. Amen.

Court Cases

The LORD loves righteousness and justice;
the earth is full of his unfailing love.
PSALM 33:5

Pray for those awaiting court dates, for families of all involved, for judges and jurors to see clearly and be unbiased, for protection of the innocent, and for God's mercy and justice. Also pray for organizations in your community that offer legal counsel to those in need.

Father, I lift up my local judges and the cases they will be seeing this week. Uncovering the truth can be difficult, and delivering justice may often feel impossible. Provide the right jurors and witnesses for each case. Give strength and clarity to the lawyers involved. Help them do their jobs with excellence. For those awaiting trial, may they receive justice and Your mercy. Reach hearts with Your love and bring glory to Your name through Your work in each case. For innocent families and children affected by the cases, bring comfort, and support and remove feelings of shame. Provide for their financial and physical needs during this disruptive time. Thank You for the organizations offering legal help for those in need. Provide wisdom and finances for their ministry and bless their efforts. In the midst of the uncertainty and waiting, may all involved know Your unfailing love. Amen.

Caregivers

Come to me, all you who are weary and burdened,
and I will give you rest. Take my yoke upon you
and learn from me, for I am gentle and humble in heart,
and you will find rest for your souls.

MATTHEW 11:28–29

Pray for caretakers of ill loved ones and for organizations that provide long-term care for those battling illness or in need of end-of-life care. Pray for those who care for loved ones with mental illness, who are raising children who have been abandoned or have special needs.

Father, thank You for the faithful individuals caring for loved ones. Day in and day out they pour out mercy and concern. When they are weary, please give them rest. Show them in small and big ways that as they serve their loved one, they are serving You. Give them moments with their loved one that are filled with joy in the midst of stress or grief. Bring someone to offer respite and pour Your love and compassion into them. Thank You for professionals who offer assistance for long-term and end-of-life care. Give them compassion, gentleness, and wisdom to offer the best comfort to the patient and caregivers. May all know You as the gentle Burden Bearer and see how You are with them. Amen.

Creator

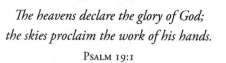

The heavens declare the glory of God;
the skies proclaim the work of his hands.

PSALM 19:1

Praise God for His wonderful, creative work. Take time to list what you have enjoyed and observed in nature and how He has created good things in your life.

Father, You are a magnificent Creator. The heavens show Your glory; the skies shout the work of Your hands. The morning sunrise is a beautiful masterpiece, and the sunset displays the brilliance of Your grandeur. I see Your hand in the flowers, in the fall colors, in a baby's head of hair. You are the most imaginative, creative Being who has ever existed. I am in awe of the beauty Your work displays around me every day. I see Your creative work in the cities, in the expanse of the fields, and in the details of my life. You create beauty out of bruises, bring calm out of chaos, and call light out of darkness. I am in continual awe of Your creative power in nature, my life, and the lives of those around me. Amen.

Comforter

You who are my Comforter in sorrow,
my heart is faint within me.

JEREMIAH 8:18

Praise God as the Great Comforter. List the ways you have experienced His care and comfort in the midst of your sorrows and heartache. Remember those times, having faith that God will comfort you now.

Father, You are the great Comforter. When I am desperate, without hope, and lost in the storm of grief, You guard my heart and mind with peace (Philippians 4:7). When I do not know what to do or even how to pray, Your Holy Spirit intercedes for me with groans I cannot understand (Romans 8:26). In all my trials and heartaches, I trust that You are present and look to You for comfort. You are my help. Even when I cannot sense Your presence, I know You do not leave me alone and call me back to Yourself. I am in awe of You and that You would take notice of my pain. You see every hurt, heartache, and sorrow. I am grateful for the wholeness You provide in the midst of my uncertainty and fear. I rest in the comfort of Your loving arms today. Amen.

Depression and Mental Health

Why, my soul, are you downcast?
Why so disturbed within me? Put your hope in God,
for I will yet praise him, my Savior and my God.

PSALM 42:11

———————————

Pray for those who suffer from depression, anxiety, and other mental health issues. Pray for their families, service providers, and for greater understanding of these illnesses.

———————————

Father, I bring before You those who battle depression, anxiety, bipolar disorder, and other mental health struggles, and those who hide their pain. I ask that they might not feel isolated and alone. Grant them courage to seek help, and the ability to accept help when it is offered. Help each one know Your love through the people who surround them. Heal their infirmities. Give them a sound mind. Let Your Holy Spirit fill their souls. Give me eyes to see those who struggle around me. Help me know how to provide encouragement and support in ways they can receive. May our Christian communities be safe places for people to share their mental or emotional needs, and may they not fear judgment or criticism. Please continue to provide greater understanding of these illnesses. Amen.

Divorce

A gentle answer turns away wrath,
but a harsh word stirs up anger.
PROVERBS 15:1

———————————

Pray for couples in your community who are considering divorce, going through the proceedings, or whose divorces are final, as they adjust to this new season of life. Pray for any children involved to know God's comfort, for reconciliation wherever possible, and for harmful words and actions to be withheld.

———————————

Father, I lift up the couples and families who are considering divorce or are going through the process. Protect their children's hearts and minds and help them to know it's not their fault. During this confusing, painful time, bring Your peace and presence as only You can do. If there is a path to reconciliation, please make it clear. If one of them is holding on to bitterness or hatred, help them release it to You. When they are feeling broken and distraught, help them sense Your love. For families adjusting to a new reality, remove any shame they may feel and provide wisdom as they establish new routines. Protect them from judgmental comments, and surround them with a community of support in the days and years to come. May they know Your grace and love and extend forgiveness whenever needed. Amen.

Dementia and Alzheimer's

Therefore we do not lose heart.
Though outwardly we are wasting away,
yet inwardly we are being renewed day by day.
2 Corinthians 4:16

Pray for individuals and their families who are suffering from dementia and Alzheimer's. Pray for strength and grace for their families and caregivers, and wisdom for challenging health-care decisions.

Father, I lift up the individuals who suffer from dementia and Alzheimer's. May they remember the truth of Your love deep inside their memory. Provide peace, comfort, and connection to You through Scriptures and songs they may have learned long ago. Please give their families hope and joy through these moments of remembering. Help all involved know that even though they may forget, You always remember them. I praise You, for though the outward body may waste away, You hold their spirits—their inner persons—in Your hand. One day, You will make them whole again. When their family and caregivers are exhausted, emotionally spent, and frustrated by their behaviors, give them Your grace and patience. Provide wisdom for the challenging but necessary health-care and safety decisions they must make. Help all involved know on a deep and personal level how much You will always love them. Amen.

Deliverer

*The LORD is my rock, my fortress and my deliverer;
my God is my rock, in whom I take refuge,
my shield and the horn of my salvation, my stronghold.*

PSALM 18:2

———————

Praise God as the Deliverer who sets His people free. Name the areas in your life in which He has released you from the power of sin, and thank Him for how He is working in the areas where you still struggle. Write them down, and mark them as reminders of what God has done for you personally and in your community.

———————

Father, You are the Great Deliverer. You sent Your Son, Jesus, to set me free from the power of sin and death. No matter what struggle or battle comes my way, You are with me. I give praise for the deliverance You've granted in the various areas of my life. I thank You that even though I still struggle in this body of flesh, You are greater than my struggle and are still working Your deliverance in my life. I offer praise for how You have brought Your deliverance in the midst of challenging situations in my community. Because of You, we can set aside selfishness for service and fear for faith. You are our Rock, our Salvation, and our Stronghold. Amen.

Dwelling Place

Lord, you have been our dwelling place throughout
all generations. Before the mountains were born
or you brought forth the whole world,
from everlasting to everlasting you are God.

PSALM 90:1–2

Praise God for being your safe haven, a place of refuge, and your "home." Ask for His help to remember He is with you as you go about your day. Praise Him for all the ways He has brought His presence and peace into your life.

Father, You are my safe place—not my job, my family, or even the work I do for You. Help me stay with You, residing in Your presence as I go about my everyday life. When struggles and temptations cross my path today and when the pace gets hectic, help me remember to come back to You. I realize that even though my body dwells in the physical world, my spirit resides with You. May my one desire be like the Psalmist's who said, "One thing I ask from the LORD, this only do I seek: that I may dwell in the house of the LORD all the days of my life" (Psalm 27:4). Amen.

Estranged Relationships

Bear with each other and forgive one another
if any of you has a grievance against someone.
Forgive as the Lord forgave you.

COLOSSIANS 3:13

———————————

Pray for families and friends with estranged relationships—husband to wife, parent to child, siblings, grandparents to grandchildren, and extended families. Pray for friends who are at odds with each other, who have felt betrayed, or where jealousy or bitterness has taken root. In these and other estranged relationships, pray for healing and forgiveness.

———————————

Father, sometimes the people who are closest to us are the ones who wound us the most. I lift up these estranged relationships. I ask for Your grace and mercy to flood these relationships. I boldly ask for restoration and that You will pave the way for healthy, respectful relationships. I ask You to fill the void in the hearts of those hurting and bring others who will be part of the healing process. Enable all to move forward in grace and peace. Convict hearts of bitterness and resentment and show us all how to release our hurts to You. Remind us how Your forgiveness through Jesus set the example for us. Help us see each other the way You see us. Amen.

Emergency Responders

He gives strength to the weary
and increases the power of the weak.

ISAIAH 40:29

Pray for the emergency responders in your community, including those working in area fire departments and ambulance crews. Pray for their safety, health, and families.

Father, thank You for the emergency responders in my community. Thank You for how they serve my community by being ready to help in our most challenging times. Give them strength and courage as they face situations that may be horrific. Provide calm and the ability to think clearly and with quick recall of their training. Help them work as a team to communicate effectively and to support each other. When they face danger, be their safe place. When they face exhaustion, give them Your strength to finish the job. As they go home to their families, help them be present as a spouse, parent, and friend. Should they struggle or be upset with what they have seen and experienced, provide safe places for them to talk and experience healing. Amen.

Elderly

Even to your old age and gray hairs I am he,
I am he who will sustain you.
I have made you and I will carry you;
I will sustain you and I will rescue you.

ISAIAH 46:4

Pray for the elderly in your community, for the families who care for them, and for the caregivers who assist them, whether at home or in assisted-living or nursing homes. Pray they will be honored and blessed until the end of their days on earth.

Father, I bring the elderly in my community before You today. Thank You for the long life You have granted them. Help us as a community let them know we value them, their wisdom, and their experiences. I ask that they would be honored and blessed until the end of their time on this earth. As they endure bodies and minds breaking down with time, grant them courage to face each day. May they remember that You are the God who made them, and You still sustain them. Should they experience loneliness, may they know You are always with them. Prompt a family member or friend to visit, call, or write. Surround them with people who patiently care for and unselfishly serve them. Be with the facilities offering care and assistance to the elderly in my community. May the staff serve the residents today with grace, patience, and dignity. Amen.

Eternal One

The eternal God is your refuge,
and underneath are the everlasting arms.

DEUTERONOMY 33:27

Praise God for His eternity. Remember how He was with you yesterday, praise Him for being with you today, and acknowledge that He already sees tomorrow. Praise God for the eternal life you have with Him as a child of God through the saving grace of Jesus Christ.

Father, You are the great Eternal One. You have no beginning and no end, for You are everlasting. Many things come and go, but You always have been and always will be. While I see such a small piece of the world's history, You see and know all. Thank You for how You were with me yesterday. Thank You for being with me today as I face my specific situations. I give praise that You see tomorrow, and no matter what I encounter or what happens in the world, You are already there. I trust You are working all things together for good, and are advancing Your eternal plan for Your glory (Romans 8:28). Thank You for sending Your Son, Jesus, so I might share eternal life with You in heaven. Amen.

Eye Opener

Open my eyes that I may see wonderful things in your law.
PSALM 119:18

Praise God for being the One who opens our eyes to who He is. Praise Him for how He has helped you understand His Word and for how He has revealed sin in your life and replaced it with His truth.

Father, I praise You for opening my eyes to the truth of who You are: the one, true God, holy and perfect, yet gracious and loving. My Savior and Redeemer, I praise You for opening my eyes and helping me understand Your words of truth. Without You, I would not comprehend the greatness of the Bible or what it means for my life. Without You, I wouldn't know the great gift of salvation You have given through Your Son, Jesus. Thank You for how You have revealed sin in my life, for Your forgiveness, and for strength to walk according to Your Word and Spirit, and not according to my sinful desires. Please continue to open my eyes today, so I may live according to Your truth. Amen.

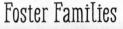

Foster Families

*Whoever welcomes one of these little children
in my name welcomes me; and whoever welcomes me
does not welcome me but the one who sent me.*

MARK 9:37

Pray for foster parents, children in the foster care system, parents who are reuniting with their children, and parents who have lost their parental rights. Pray for all care providers—social workers, therapists, teachers, caseworkers, and judges. Ask God to raise up more foster families in your community.

Father, thank You for those who open their homes as foster parents. Please give them wisdom and patience as they love the children in their homes and work with social workers and biological parents through complicated situations. Enable them to give each child the time and attention he or she needs. Provide support for their practical needs. Be with each child as they transition, whether to a foster home or to their own. Let them feel loved and know they are not alone. Raise up more families willing to offer respite, love, and care. Give judges and social workers and their agencies clarity for what is best for the children. Be with each biological parent who is trying to reunite their family, and minister to those who have lost rights to their children. Let them know that You have not abandoned them. Help each child experience Your love through their foster families. Amen.

Forgiveness

Forgive us our sins, for we also forgive everyone
who sins against us. And lead us not into temptation.

LUKE 11:4

Pray that forgiveness would be a primary trait in your life and community, remembering how Christ came to forgive and taught us to forgive one another. Ask God to shine His light into your heart and reveal any unforgiveness you are holding on to.

Father, help me not hold on to offenses but to forgive quickly. Search my heart and reveal any unforgiveness I have clung to. Clear my heart of bitterness, anger, and resentment. Fill me with Your love for those who have wounded me, whether present offenses or those from long ago. I recognize forgiveness is not something I can do in my own strength, but through Your Spirit's help. When someone speaks a careless word, help me give it to You immediately. When someone intentionally hurts me, show me what it means to forgive as You forgave me. Help my community be one known for forgiveness. When our community is hurt—whether in our churches, neighborhoods, or schools—give us the grace and strength to respond in a way that will bring honor to You. Amen.

Finances

Keep your lives free from the love of money
and be content with what you have, because God has said,
"Never will I leave you; never will I forsake you."

Hebrews 13:5

––––––––––––––––––

Pray over your finances and for those you know who struggle financially. Pray your community will keep free from the love of money, learn contentedness, and recognize that God will never leave them, even during financial trouble.

––––––––––––––––––

Father, forgive me for where I have allowed the love of money to creep into my life. Help me remember to put my trust in You—not in a bank account, in possessions, or in what money can do for me. Let my security rest in You, not my stuff. Help me learn to be content with what I have, and not always be searching for the next great thing. Grow my desire to use money to serve You and Your kingdom. Please be with individuals and families who are struggling financially. Help all remember You will never leave or abandon them. Prevent shame. Give strength and wisdom for hard decisions. Provide for needs in ways that can be attributed only to You. As a community, help us recognize where love of money has replaced our love for You. Help us remember that money is a tool to serve You and a gift to provide for our needs. Amen.

He is the Rock, his works are perfect, and all his ways are just.
A faithful God who does no wrong, upright and just is he.

DEUTERONOMY 32:4

Praise God for His faithfulness in your life and community. Remember how He has been faithful even when you have not. List ways He has been faithful to His promises, not just to you but toward all.

Father, You are a faithful God who does no wrong. You are perfect, holy, and just. Your goodness to humanity amazes me. Faithfulness surrounds You, is part of who You are, and is not dependent on my faithfulness to You (Psalm 89:8). You have been faithful to Your promises in the Scriptures. You remembered Your covenant to Abraham, Isaac, and Jacob. Even when their children were not faithful, You always were. You remembered Your love for Your people and sent the ultimate Redeemer, Your Son. Through Him, You called us into fellowship with Yourself (1 Corinthians 1:9). There is no god like You. None so faithful. None so true. You are the one, true, faithful God. Amen.

Future-Holder

I make known the end from the beginning,
from ancient times, what is still to come.
I say, "My purpose will stand, and I will do all that I please."
ISAIAH 46:10

Praise God that He holds the future in His hands. Recognize that while the future often seems uncertain or tenuous, He is working His plan in all of creation, and His purpose will stand. Place your future and your community's future in His hands.

Father, You are the only One who sees tomorrow, and You tell us not to worry about it (Matthew 6:34). Yet it's often hard to obey that command. I praise You for the plan You are working through all of history. I praise You that Your purposes will stand. No matter what happens with world leaders or natural disasters, You will do all You please. Not a thing is out of Your control. I place these things about my future and my community's future in Your hands. Thank You that I don't need to worry about it, try to control it, or make it work out on my own power. You know the beginning and the end, and I place my life and my trust in You. Amen.

Grieving

*The LORD is close to the brokenhearted
and saves those who are crushed in spirit.*

PSALM 34:18

Pray for those who grieve and for those who are watching a loved one in their last stages of life. Pray also for those grieving change or other losses—health, relationships, or transitions in life.

Father, I bring to You those who are grieving. May all know You as the God of comfort, the God who sees, the God who never leaves us or forsakes us. May loving arms surround them, and in quiet moments alone, may they know You are still there. Help them not to stuff their emotions, but to feel them and move through the grief. Help them come to You in their lament with openness and honesty about their deep grief. Enable them to grieve at their own pace, to take care of themselves, and give them grace as they adjust to a new "normal." Give their community wisdom to know when to reach out and when to give space. May all who grieve know the joy that comes in the morning after a long time of darkness. Amen.

Gratitude

Rejoice always, pray continually,
give thanks in all circumstances;
for this is God's will for you in Christ Jesus.

1 Thessalonians 5:16–18

Ask God to help you and your community express gratitude in all circumstances. Name specific situations in your life and community that are good and others that are challenging. Express gratitude for who God is and how you see His hand in each setting.

Father, it's easy to give thanks when life is full of good things and when I don't have to hunt for the blessings. It can also be easy to forget to give thanks when life is good and things are going well. Help me remember to stop and give thanks in all circumstances—the good and easy and the challenging. I give praise for these good things in my life. And in the midst of these challenging situations, I give thanks for how I see You working and for who You are. Every good and perfect gift comes from You (James 1:17). Help my community recognize this truth and learn to express gratitude in all circumstances. Open our eyes to recognize the good gifts we can be grateful for in each situation we encounter. Amen.

Generosity

A generous person will prosper;
whoever refreshes others will be refreshed.

PROVERBS 11:25

Ask God to reveal how you can show generosity in your community, not just with your finances and possessions, but also with your time and abilities. Pray your community would be generous in all situations.

Father, everything I own belongs to You—my time, talents, and possessions have all come from You. Show me how I can be generous in offering my specific things and talents to You by serving others. Prompt me by Your Spirit to recognize the opportunities You place in front of me to do good to all people, especially those who are part of Your family (Galatians 6:10). When I feel like I don't have the time or energy or resources to be generous, remind me that You sent Jesus, who gave up everything for me. Remind me how in refreshing others I will also be refreshed. I pray for my community to be one of great generosity. May we take care of each other and offer everything we have in generous service to each other in Your name and for Your glory. Amen.

Graciousness

The LORD is gracious and righteous;
our God is full of compassion.
PSALM 116:5

Praise God for His graciousness in your life. Recall the times when He did not give you what you deserved but instead displayed His grace, particularly through the gift of salvation in Jesus.

Father, You are a gracious and compassionate God. You understand that I am but flesh (Psalm 78:38–39). You are slow to anger and overflowing with love and faithfulness. I give praise for how You've given the gift of grace through Jesus—a gift I cannot earn and can never repay (Ephesians 2:8–9). You have offered grace and not given the judgment I deserved so many times. Your grace preserves my life and sustains me every day, even when I do not realize it. I praise You for Your compassionate understanding of me and my weaknesses. Thank You for helping me grow to be more like Your Son. You have shown Your grace in my community in many ways. There is no one so understanding as You. Help me and my community be a reflection of Your grace to all we encounter. May our gracious extension of Your love bring people to You. Amen.

Greatness

Sovereign LORD, you have begun to show to your servant
your greatness and your strong hand.
For what god is there in heaven or on earth who can do
the deeds and mighty works you do?

Deuteronomy 3:24

Praise God for His greatness. Recall how you see His greatness in creation, in the work He does in your life and in those around you. List the deeds and mighty works you have seen Him do.

Father, I cannot even begin to comprehend Your greatness. So much trouble and strife and struggle exist in this world, but You are greater than this world and its enemy (1 John 4:4). No one can do the works You have done. You have defeated death and sin. You fashioned the highest mountains and carved the depths of the sea. You paint Your majesty in the sunset, sound Your power in the crashing of the ocean's waves, and soar Your glory through the birds in the sky. I see Your greatness in my life. I see Your greatness in my community. You will reign forever, and no power of darkness can stop You. You are the one, true, great God who is always victorious. Amen.

Homeless

*You have been a refuge for the poor, a refuge for the needy in
their distress, a shelter from the storm and a shade from the heat.*

<small>Isaiah 25:4</small>

Pray for those in need of housing and for their physical, emotional, and mental health needs to be met through community
organizations. Pray for those who are homeless because they
are fleeing unsafe situations. Pray for protection for children
who are homeless and for provision for the organizations that
serve the homeless.

Father, please forgive me for how I have failed to care for the
homeless in my community. Give me eyes to see as You do.
Strip me of stereotypes, and show me how I can offer love and
practical assistance in helpful ways. For those living without
adequate shelter, please provide safe places to sleep. Give refuge from the weather and help them find food. Provide the
skills they need to have a better, sustainable quality of life.
Grant safety and protection to those fleeing unsafe situations.
Be with teachers who have homeless children in their class-
rooms, and be with homeless teens without support. Help my
community find ways to be Your hands and feet of love to the
homeless. Thank You for the organizations serving the homeless in my community. Provide adequate resources and give
wisdom as they assist individuals and families in need. Amen.

Heart Disease

*Is anyone among you sick? Let them call the elders of the church
to pray over them and anoint them with oil in the name
of the Lord. And the prayer offered in faith will make
the sick person well; the Lord will raise them up.*

JAMES 5:14–15

Pray for those in your community who battle heart disease, for early detection, for any upcoming surgeries and recovery, for the doctors and nurses offering treatment and a recovery plan, and for their families.

Father, thank You for the advances You have granted in heart care and for the hospitals offering heart care in my community. Please be with these individuals and their families who are battling heart disease. Give them peace and courage as they face surgery and recovery. Provide the doctors with wisdom regarding a treatment plan. Surround the patient and family with a supportive community through the long recovery process. Help them grow in discipline to implement any needed lifestyle changes. Protect them from depression and discouragement as they adjust to a new way of life. Guard their hearts from fear about the future. You are the One who created our hearts and bodies, and I offer them back to You, the great Healer and Physician. Amen.

Hunger

He upholds the cause of the oppressed
and gives food to the hungry.
PSALM 146:7

Pray for those in your community who do not have enough to eat. Pray for the organizations who serve them to have sufficient means to meet the needs of your community, and the ability to connect their services with those who need it. Pray for parents who need insight for providing for their families in a land of plenty and for sustainable solutions for each family.

Father, You are the God who makes it rain and causes our food to grow. I ask You to provide sufficient food for those in my community who are not able to feed their families. Give me eyes to see needs and the ability to help. Give insight and sustainable solutions for parents struggling to provide enough food for their families. Thank You for the organizations serving the hungry in my community. Provide enough resources in the form of money, food, and volunteers so they may have sufficient means to meet the great needs in the community. Prompt churches and families to get involved. Help us realize it's not just a problem for the organizations to solve but understand how we can all be part of the solution. Thank You for upholding the cause of the oppressed and feeding the hungry. Amen.

Holy, holy, holy is the LORD Almighty;
the whole earth is full of his glory.

ISAIAH 6:3

Praise God for His absolute holiness. Praise Him as the holy God who desires fellowship with you and provided the way through Jesus.

Father, You are the holy Lord God Almighty. The whole earth is filled with Your glory. You are the perfect, pure, sinless God. No one compares to Your majesty and glory. You are the holy God about whom the angels continuously declare, "'Holy, holy, holy is the Lord God Almighty, who was, and is, and is to come'" (Revelation 4:8). You, the holy God, loved me so much You provided a way for me to have a relationship with You through the sacrifice of Your Son, Jesus. I could never approach You on my own. Sin stained my life, but You washed it away through Jesus' blood. That a holy God would desire me is a gift I cannot comprehend, but one I am grateful for. Words cannot express the fullness of Your glory and holiness. You are the holy, mighty God. Amen.

Helper

So we say with confidence, "The Lord is my helper;
I will not be afraid. What can mere mortals do to me?"

HEBREWS 13:6

Praise God as your Helper. Recall the ways He has helped you in the past and how you see His help in situations today.

Father, You are my Helper. Because of Your help, I do not need to be afraid of what people can do to me, of the evils the world holds, or the danger I may face today. You are with me, and You never forsake me (Hebrews 13:5). Jesus promised His followers they would not be left as orphans, and You sent the Holy Spirit to be our Helper (John 14:18). Thank You for how the Spirit teaches us and reminds us of Your words and promises (John 14:26). Thank You for all the ways You have helped me in the past. I praise You for how You are helping me in my current situations. Make Your work evident in my life and in my community. No matter what we face, may we always remember we are not alone and say with confidence, "You, God, are my Helper." Amen.

Infertility

In the same way, the Spirit helps us in our weakness.
We do not know what we ought to pray for, but the Spirit
himself intercedes for us through wordless groans.

ROMANS 8:26

Pray for those struggling to have children, those undergoing fertility treatments, those who've had unsuccessful treatments, and for those who've suffered miscarriages and stillbirths.

Father, I bring my friends to You who desire children, yet are unable so far to have them. My heart aches, words fail me, and I do not understand. Yet You never fail. Draw all in these situations close to You. Give a hope and trust in You that will never fade. When darkness overwhelms, when all hope seems lost, when careless words are spoken, may they know the light of Your love. Protect marriages and relationships with any other children in the family. Be with siblings who may not understand. Please provide a supportive community and wisdom for difficult decisions. Encourage them not to withdraw from the people who love them, but to let them journey with them through the pain. In the years to come when the ache washes over them anew, be their peace that passes understanding. Amen.

Incarceration

When did we see you sick or in prison and go to visit you?
The King will reply, "Truly I tell you, whatever you did for one
of the least of these brothers and sisters of mine, you did for me."

MATTHEW 25:39–40

Pray for those in prison in your community and for their families. Pray God will protect the hearts of their children and that He would heal the pain and answer the questions they have. Pray for those working in the prison system, from the administrators to the guards. Pray for ministries in your community that work with prisoners to bring hope and healing and the message of Christ.

Father, I bring before You those incarcerated in my community. Provide hope and encouragement for each of them and their families today. Be with their children; heal their pain and answer their questions. Provide a supportive community for those transitioning back into society. Help restore their lives and rebuild their families. Give strength to cut ties with any harmful relationships that would lead to old ways of living. Please be with the individuals and organizations that serve prisoners. Provide wisdom as they counsel the incarcerated and their families. Within my local prisons provide protection for the employees; may they operate out of integrity and wisdom. Amen.

Idolatry

*Put to death, therefore, whatever belongs to your earthly nature:
sexual immorality, impurity, lust,
evil desires and greed, which is idolatry.*

COLOSSIANS 3:5

Pray for your life and community to be free from idolatry and that God would take first place in your life. Ask for eyes to see what things have become idols in your life.

Father, You commanded Your people not to place any other gods before You (Exodus 20:3). The things I put my trust in above You aren't as easy to identify as idols made of wood or stone. Help me recognize things that have replaced You as the source of my security, hope, and purpose; and enable me through the power of Your Holy Spirit to eradicate those things from my life. I confess that even good things can become an idol, like my knowledge of Your Word or even my service to You. Keep my heart pure and wash away destructive pride and desires in my life. Convict my community of things we have elevated above You. Reveal our idolatry and move us to confession and repentance. May our first desire always be for You. Amen.

Infiniteness

*"Who can hide in secret places so that
I cannot see them?" declares the LORD.
"Do not I fill heaven and earth?" declares the LORD.*

JEREMIAH 23:24

Praise God as infinite—endless, unlimited, and immeasurably great. Praise Him for His infinite power and presence in your life and community.

Father, there is nowhere I can go where You are not there. No one can measure the size of Your presence or the scope of Your power. You fill not only the entire earth, but heaven as well. You, see everything, and there are no secrets You do not already know. The great King Solomon hesitated to build a temple for You, claiming the highest heavens can't even contain You, so how could You possibly dwell among people? (2 Chronicles 2:6; 6:2). Yet You chose to dwell among people through Your Son and Your Spirit. When I am lost, lonely, and lacking wisdom, You offer comfort, companionship, and courage. I praise You for the infinite power and wisdom You have shown in my life. Your infinite power shows itself even in the darkest times in our community. Thank You for filling every space above, below, around, and within me. Amen.

Infallible God

The law of the LORD is perfect, refreshing the soul.
The statutes of the LORD are trustworthy,
making wise the simple.

PSALM 19:7

––––––––––––––

Praise God and His Word as absolutely trustworthy, sure, reliable, and unfailing. Thank God that while people may fail you, He never will.

––––––––––––––

Father, You are the infallible God. You are completely trustworthy and sure. Your Word is reliable and unfailing and refreshes my soul. Your way is perfect and Your law is flawless (Psalm 18:30). Your Word is eternal and stands firm in the heavens (Psalm 119:89). I delight in Your Word, for it guides, protects, and leads me in the way I should go. I praise You for how You have revealed Yourself through Your Word and how Your Word works in my everyday life. Even when I doubt You, You are steady and unmoved. When I do not sense Your presence or understand Your plan, You are still working Your good and perfect will in the world. I give praise that while people will fail me, You never will. Amen.

Job Seekers

*Whatever you do, work at it with all your heart,
as working for the Lord, not for human masters, since you know
that you will receive an inheritance from the Lord as a reward.
It is the Lord Christ you are serving.*

Colossians 3:23–24

Pray for the unemployed, the underemployed, and those who need better jobs. Pray for patience and endurance as they seek employment, and the understanding that a job does not define their worth.

Father, I bring my friends to You who need jobs. During this season, may they clearly see how You are providing for their every need. Help them trust You and Your timing during this painful waiting. Draw them closer to You, and may they find their identity through Your Word. Help them remember their value does not rest in a paycheck, but in the price You have already paid for them through Christ. I ask You to bless them with meaningful work that provides for their needs in Your perfect timing. Give them courage to ask for help, and open my eyes to see how I can serve them in ways they can receive. In the end, may they know Your hand has never left them. Help us all remember that our jobs do not define us, but You do. Amen.

Jealousy

You desire but do not have, so you kill. You covet
but you cannot get what you want, so you quarrel and fight.
You do not have because you do not ask God.

JAMES 4:2

Pray against jealousy in your life and community. Recognize where you struggle with jealousy and ask for God's help through His Holy Spirit. Pray that your community would not be overcome with jealousy but would instead celebrate each other's successes.

Father, jealousy is a silent thief. It steals happiness, joy, and contentedness with the gifts You have given. Jealousy wrecks relationships and causes arguments. Please forgive me for the times I have been jealous of the good gifts You have given others. Help me be aware of jealous thoughts as soon as they happen and through Your Spirit replace them with prayers of blessing and gratitude for the other person. Help me not covet what I do not have and instead be thankful for all You have already given me. Please help my community not be overcome with jealousy—whether it be of material gain, relationships, or successes. Help us celebrate the achievements, benefits, and opportunities You give to each of us. May we be a community of encouragement and prayer, not of jealous quarrels and fights. Amen.

Joy

For the joy of the LORD is your strength.
NEHEMIAH 8:10

Pray that you and your community would be filled with God's joy. Recognize how joy is not dependent on circumstances, but comes from the Lord and His salvation and is a fruit of the Spirit.

Father, my heart takes joy in You and Your salvation. When my heart mourns and weeps over heartbreaking situations, remind me that Your joy comes in the morning (Psalm 30:5). While happiness may fade with circumstances, Your joy is deep, is unending, and is my strength. Please fill my heart with joy when darkness overwhelms me. Remind me how Your salvation cannot be taken away. Grow the fruit of joy in my life through Your Holy Spirit (Galatians 5:22). Help my community be one of joy, even during the most trying situations. Help us remember You are our inheritance. Keep our eyes on You and show us the path of life. Remind us that with You at our right hand we cannot be shaken. Fill us with joy in Your presence (Psalm 16:8, 11). Amen.

Jehovah-Jireh

So Abraham called that place The LORD Will Provide.
And to this day it is said,
"On the mountain of the LORD it will be provided."

GENESIS 22:14

———————

Praise God as Jehovah-Jireh, which is the name given to God by Abraham when God provided a ram as a sacrifice instead of his son Isaac. Praise God for how He has provided for needs in your life and community and for the sacrifice of Jesus.

———————

Father, You are the great God who provides. Just as You provided the ram as a sacrifice instead of Abraham's son, Isaac, You provided the sacrifice for my sins through Your Son, Jesus. I praise You for how the gift of salvation and forgiveness of sin has changed my life. You are the God who also provides for physical needs. You provided food and water for Your people in the desert. You provided protection from their enemies and a land flowing with milk and honey for their home. I praise You for how You provide for my needs. I praise You for how You have provided for the needs of my community—for the protection You have granted and for how You have provided Your presence during times of trouble. You are the God who always provides what we need. I give praise for how You grow my faith when provision seems delayed or denied. I trust You as my Provider. Amen.

Justice

Yet the LORD longs to be gracious to you;
therefore he will rise up to show you compassion.
For the LORD is a God of justice.
Blessed are all who wait for him!

Isaiah 30:18

Praise God that He is just. He is righteous, is impartial, is upright, and does no wrong. Praise Him for the justice He provides in all situations, that vengeance is His, and that He will take care of injustices in your life (Romans 12:19).

Father, You are fair, righteous, and just. All Your works are perfect, and You do no wrong. Yet You long to be gracious to us and show us compassion—a truth that brings me to my knees in gratitude. I praise You for how You have brought justice in my life. I praise You for the justice You have provided in my community. I place my trust in You and believe You will right the injustices happening in my life and community. Vengeance is Yours, and I praise You that I do not need to worry or solve the issues on my own. Thank You that Your work on earth is not yet done and You continue to mend the world. One day You will wipe away every tear (Revelation 7:17). I will wait for You and Your justice. Amen.

Kindness

*But the fruit of the Spirit is love, joy, peace, forbearance,
kindness, goodness, faithfulness, gentleness and self-control.
Against such things there is no law.*

GALATIANS 5:22–23

Pray that you and your community will be filled with and known for kindness and compassion.

Father, I desire to display the fruit of kindness, yet sometimes I don't know how to do so. Through Your Holy Spirit, please grow this fruit in me until it overflows into the lives around me. Prompt me with practical ideas to reach out and offer Your loving-kindness to those around me every day. When I am the one in need, help me humbly open the door and allow the kindness of others into my life. Begin a movement of kindness in my community that catches and spreads. May we show kindness, not for recognition or a good feeling, but quietly, out of love and appreciation for the kindness You have shown us. Show us this week who needs a smile, a gesture, or a helping hand. Give us courage to act and not to expect anything in return. Amen.

Knowledge of God

The fear of the LORD is the beginning of wisdom,
and knowledge of the Holy One is understanding.

PROVERBS 9:10

Pray for you and your community to be filled with the knowledge of God and His Word through the teaching in local churches and the testimony of believers, and for those seeking God to come to know Him.

Father, the fear of You—my reverence, openness, and obedience to You—is the beginning of wisdom and knowledge. Knowledge of You and Your Word brings strength, hope, and peace for all I face. The heavens speak of Your glory and reveal knowledge of You (Psalm 19:1–2). The wisdom, knowledge, and understanding You give is sweet to my soul (Proverbs 2:6, 10). I desire to seek You and Your knowledge each day. May my community be one that openly teaches the knowledge of You and Your Word. Be present in these bodies of believers, and may their teachings reveal the knowledge of You and Your Word. As their attendees go about their lives in the community, may each person spread the knowledge of You by how he or she lives. Provide those who seek You an example of what You are like by how Your followers live. Help us all be obedient to You and Your Word. Amen.

Keeping the Faith

I have fought the good fight, I have finished the race,
I have kept the faith.

2 TIMOTHY 4:7

Pray that you and your community would keep the faith for the duration of your life. Ask for help to remain obedient and faithful in areas of struggle and for strength to resist temptation to give up the faith.

Father, sometimes I get tired of the fight. Sometimes I am weary of running the race, and exhaustion overtakes me. It is tempting to give up when the whole world seems against Your followers. When the end of my life approaches, I desire the quiet confidence of knowing I have done all You have asked of me. I want to live a faithful and obedient life and not run away when the challenge is too hard or give in to my old sinful ways. I look forward to the crown of righteousness and desire to live a life worthy of it (2 Timothy 4:8). As a community, give us strength to endure the challenges before us and help us keep the faith. May we be a shining light for You, fight the enemy well, and remember that our battle is not against flesh and blood, but against the powers of this dark world and spiritual forces of evil (Ephesians 6:12). Help us stand together in faith and be obedient until the very end. Amen.

King of Kings

On his robe and on his thigh he has this name written:
KING OF KINGS AND LORD OF LORDS.

Revelation 19:16

Praise God as the King above all kings and the Lord of all lords. Recognize how He is King of your life and community.

Father, You are the King of all kings and Lord of all lords. Jesus said You gave all authority in heaven and earth to Him (Matthew 28:18). Nothing in this world happens without Your notice. Even though world powers and rulers may not recognize You now, one day they will all confess You as their King and Lord, and You will rule forever and ever. I submit to Your authority and power. Be the Lord of my life. Show me the way to go and help me follow You every step of the day. Help my community recognize You as the King of their lives. Help us show the world what it means to live as a community in submission to Your authority, and may others be drawn to You through our lives of obedience to Your will. Amen.

Keeper of My Soul

The LORD is your keeper;
The LORD is your shade at your right hand.
PSALM 121:5 NKJV

Praise God as the One who keeps your soul in this life and the life to come. Recall the ways He has kept you in the past and how He continues to keep you today.

Father, You are the one who keeps me, not just in this life, but also in the life to come. I rest in Your hands. You have given eternal life so I will never perish, and I am so grateful for this gift. Nothing can ever take me out of Your hand, for You are greater than all the powers of this world (John 10:28–30). I praise You that no matter what comes may way—whatever attack, trial, or trouble invades my life—You are the Keeper of my soul. You provide shade from the heat, rest for the weary, and respite for my soul when I need it most (Matthew 11:28–30). I praise You for the way You have kept me—in the past, and for how You continue to keep me—in Your hand in the midst of my situations. I trust You as my Keeper. Amen.

Lawmakers

In the LORD's hand the king's heart
is a stream of water that he channels
toward all who please him.

PROVERBS 21:1

Pray for those who make the laws—local, state, and national. Pray for legislation in process and for God to direct and guide lawmakers in the leading of the nation.

Father, I acknowledge that You hold the hearts of the rulers of all nations in Your hand. You direct, and You lead them. I ask for the lawmakers of this nation to be sensitive to Your leading, and for the laws they create to honor You. Embolden Christian politicians to stand for what is true and right and not to compromise their beliefs. Show us how to honor our leaders while at the same time honoring You. When we disagree with our laws or our politicians, help us to do so in a way that honors You, brings glory to Your name, and still shows respect for the leader's position. Amen.

Law Enforcement

Let everyone be subject to the governing authorities,
for there is no authority except that which God has established.
The authorities that exist have been established by God.
Consequently, whoever rebels against the authority is rebelling
against what God has instituted, and those who
do so will bring judgment on themselves.

ROMANS 13:1–2

Pray for your local law enforcement units for good judgment, wisdom in dealing with the community, and safety as they go about their work.

Father, thank You for my local law enforcement and their commitment to keep the community safe—police chief, detectives, and officers. Give wisdom, clarity of mind, and good judgment as they encounter stressful situations that require them to think and act quickly. Provide courage to do what is necessary for the good of the people involved. Empower the department's leadership with ideas to promote the safety of the force and the town and the ability to build trustworthy relationships with the community. Provide for their physical and emotional safety, and for the emotional health of their families. Help their hearts remain unjaded toward the people they serve and remind them of their high calling to the community and to You. Amen.

Lack of Medical Care

Then they cried to the LORD In their trouble,
and he saved them from their distress.
He sent out his word and healed them;
he rescued them from the grave.

PSALM 107:19–20

Pray for those in your community who do not have access to medical care. Pray for the hospitals and organizations in your community who are providing solutions and care for those who need it most.

Father, You have created our bodies as a beautiful, complex maze of bone and flesh to carry us through this life. Thank You for the organizations and medical systems in the community who study the body and provide care when we are sick. I pray for those in my community who do not have access to medical care when they need it, whether due to lack of finances, transportation, or not understanding the need for care. Provide access to assistance and people who will come alongside to provide care and comfort. Give insight and solutions to parents who need sustainable solutions for their family's healthcare needs. Show my community how we can remove barriers to good health care and offer medical assistance to all. Amen.

Light

In him was life, and that life was the light of all mankind.
The light shines in the darkness,
and the darkness has not overcome it.

JOHN 1:4–5

———————————

Praise God as the true Light who has overcome the darkness. Recall the ways He has brought His light into your life and community and defeated darkness.

———————————

Father, You are the Light, and in You there is no darkness (1 John 1:5). The world can seem darker than midnight, with people even loving darkness because of their evil deeds (John 3:19). But darkness will never overcome the light You have shown us through Jesus. When darkness threatens to swallow me, remind me that You are the Light of the world, and that, as I follow You, I have the Light of Life (John 8:12). I praise You for the ways Your light has come into my life and defeated darkness. May my community be one that shines Your light through good deeds that glorify You (Matthew 5:16). I look forward to the day when there will be no more night, and all nations will walk by Your light, where nothing impure, shameful, or deceitful will enter in (Revelation 21:23–27). Amen.

Love

Whoever does not love does not know God,
because God is love.

1 JOHN 4:8

Praise God for His love. Recall the ways His love has changed your life and your community.

Father, You are love. You showed the ultimate love when You sent Your only Son, Jesus, to die for my sins so I could have eternal life (John 3:16). You could have condemned me, but instead You showed me love. Your love has changed me, and I will never be the same. Your love is patient and kind, not self-seeking or easily angered. It does not keep a record of my wrongs. Your love protects, hopes, and perseveres (1 Corinthians 14:4–7). Thank You for Your unfailing love, which endures forever. I praise You that nothing—neither death nor life, angels nor demons, neither the present nor the future, nor any power, no height nor depth, or anything in all of creation—can separate me from Your love (Romans 8:38–39). There is no love like Yours. Enable me to love like You in every situation, through every trial, in times good and bad. Help my community love each other deeply as You have loved us. May the world know we are Your followers by our love for each other (John 13:34–35). Amen.

Marriages

Though one may be overpowered, two can defend themselves.
A cord of three strands is not quickly broken.

ECCLESIASTES 4:12

———————————

Pray for strong marriages in your family and community. Pray for God's intervention and restoration for those in difficult, abusive, or failing marriages. Pray for faith communities to be safe places for struggling marriages. Pray for the institution of marriage, which is under attack, and for God's covenant of marriage to bring glory to Him.

———————————

Father, help us remember that marriage was designed by You as a holy relationship that reflects our relationship with You. I praise You for how strong marriages impact generations to come and the community around us. Please strengthen the marriages in my community and family. Show them how to love each other as Christ loved the Church. Protect them from outside forces seeking to tear them apart. Help them recognize habits causing distance in their relationships. May they have a deep, personal connection with You and build a relationship together through Your Word and prayer. Bring conviction and repentance in cases of sin and infidelity. Provide strength, clarity, and safety for spouses and children in abusive marriages. Equip churches in the community to help destructive marriages. Teach our community how to support marriages and be a safe place for those who are struggling. Amen.

Missionaries and Ministers

Therefore go and make disciples of all nations,
baptizing them in the name of the Father and of the Son
and of the Holy Spirit, and teaching them to obey
everything I have commanded you.
And surely I am with you always, to the very end of the age.

MATTHEW 28:19–20

Pray for missionaries from your community, for pastors in your community, and for those involved in ministries in your area to be faithful to the teaching of the Word and shepherding the people God has entrusted to them.

Father, thank You for the individuals and families who have dedicated their lives and careers to serving the body of believers and teaching Your Word. Give them insight into Your Word and help them boldly teach the Scripture. Provide wisdom to shepherd their communities into mature and growing relationships with You. Keep them humble; may they only seek Your approval, not the approval of the people they serve. Help them lead their organizations in ways that honor You. Protect them from evil forces that would seek to destroy their families, discredit their work, and dishonor Your name. Remind them through Your Holy Spirit that You are always with them. Show us how we can support them as they serve You. Amen.

Military

God is our refuge and strength,
an ever-present help in trouble.

PSALM 46:1

Pray for the members and leadership of all branches of the military in active duty and their families. Pray for veterans as they return and adjust to life at home, and for assistance and comfort for those who carry lifelong injuries of body and mind. Pray for comfort for families who've lost loved ones in service.

Father, thank You for the members of the military who put their lives on the line for the sake of peace and freedom. Protect them as they face danger. Give them courage, strength, and wisdom to make good decisions in the heat of the moment. Provide Your peace to the veterans who are returning home, and help them and their families as they adjust to a new "normal." Give patience and support to those who suffer from injuries to their bodies and minds. Bring healing and a sound mind. Show us how we can love them, give them dignity, and honor the sacrifice they have made on our behalf. Comfort families who are grieving the loss of their loved ones. Help us walk alongside them and honor their loved ones' memories and sacrifices. Amen.

Majesty

The LORD reigns, he is robed in majesty;
the LORD is robed in majesty and armed with strength;
indeed, the world is established, firm and secure.
Your throne was established long ago; you are from all eternity.

PSALM 93:1–2

Praise God for His majesty—His supreme greatness, authority, grandeur, and rule over the universe. Recall the ways you have seen His majesty in creation and in your life.

Father, You are robed in majesty and strength. The heavens declare Your majesty, and Your glory is seen across the earth. You have established the earth and keep it firm and secure. There is no one more grand or supreme than You. From Your throne in heaven, You rule over the universe. Your throne was established long ago and is for all eternity. You have defeated Your enemies, and not even death could hold Your Son in the grave. I see Your majesty displayed in creation. I praise You for how You've shown Your majestic power in my life. There is no one more powerful and majestic than You. Amen.

Mercy

The LORD is compassionate and gracious, slow to anger,
abounding in love. He will not always accuse,
nor will he harbor his anger forever; he does not treat us
as our sins deserve or repay us according to our iniquities.

PSALM 103:8–10

Praise God for His mercy. Recall the compassion He has shown you despite your sin and the favor and blessing He has given you and your community.

Father, You are a compassionate and gracious God. You are slow to anger and abounding in love. When You could have left me accused, You provided Your mercy and forgiveness of sins. Your Son paid the price, offering full payment for my debt of sin. I praise You for the mercy You have given me. The blessing and favor You've bestowed on me is nothing I could attain for myself. I owe my life and all I am to You. I desire to live in a way that honors the price You've paid for my life. I praise You for the blessings and mercies You have given my community. Help us extend Your mercy to those around us each day. Amen.

Neighbors

The second is this: "Love your neighbor as yourself."
There is no commandment greater than these.

MARK 12:31

Pray for those who live around you, for their marriages, for their parenting, and for opportunities to love them well. Pray for protection against quarrels and for reconciliation and forgiveness to happen where there is conflict.

Father, You said the greatest two commands were to love You and to love my neighbors. Forgive me for where I fail to love my neighbors. Show me how I can do so, and grant me courage and discipline to follow through when You give me ideas for practical acts of love. I pray for my neighbors who don't know You or whose relationship with You has grown cold. Draw them to Yourself, and use me to show Your love to them. Strengthen my neighbors' marriages, and grow their desire to connect with their children in meaningful ways. I bring any tensions in my neighborhood to You and ask for grace, forgiveness, and understanding to reign. Help us be patient with each other, not to argue over petty issues, and to look out for each other's interests above our own. May Your name be honored in my neighborhood. Amen.

New Believers

We continually ask God to fill you with the knowledge
of his will through all the wisdom and understanding
that the Spirit gives, so that you may live a life worthy
of the Lord and please him in every way: bearing fruit
in every good work, growing in the knowledge of God,
being strengthened with all power according to his glorious
might so that you may have great endurance and patience.

COLOSSIANS 1:9–11

Pray for new believers in your community to grow in maturity and deepen their knowledge of God. Pray they will stand firm when they face temptation to return to their old ways of life, and ask God to show how you can come alongside them as they grow in faith. Pray that God will protect their minds and hearts from the enemy and give them a hunger for His Word.

Father, thank You for the gift of salvation and for the new members of Your family. I ask that You would fill them with Your Spirit and enable them to grow in their understanding of You. Help them follow You each day of their lives and live worthy of You, bearing good fruit in all they do. When they are tempted to return to their old way of life, surround them with a community that will encourage them to stay the course of faith. Show me how I can come alongside them in their journeys and be an example and encouragement. Amen.

Nature Care

God saw all that he had made, and it was very good. . . .
The LORD God took the man and put him
in the Garden of Eden to work it and take care of it.

GENESIS 1:31; 2:15

Pray that your community would take proper care of the earth that has been entrusted to them. Pray that families and individuals in your community will have spaces to enjoy nature in ways that will draw them to the Creator.

Father, You have created a beautiful earth and entrusted it to our care and stewardship. Forgive me for how I have neglected or abused my duties as a caretaker of the earth. Remind us that the earth and all it contains belongs to You. Prompt community leaders and businesses to protect and preserve our soil, air, water, and natural resources for our health and for the generations to come. Show us where we can reserve areas for families and individuals to escape modern life and enjoy the simple pleasures of the outdoors and connect with You. Help us care for the earth and the creatures within it as You do. Amen.

Name Above All Names

Therefore God exalted him to the highest place and gave him
the name that is above every name, that at the name
of Jesus every knee should bow, in heaven and on earth
and under the earth, and every tongue acknowledge
that Jesus Christ is Lord, to the glory of God the Father.

Philippians 2:9–11

———————————

Praise God for His name that is above all names, and that one day everyone will recognize who He is and bow to acknowledge Him as Lord. Recognize His name and authority as first place in your life.

———————————

Father, there is no one higher or greater than You. You have exalted Your Son, Jesus, to the highest place and given Him the name above every name. I look forward to the day when everyone will kneel and recognize Jesus as Lord for Your glory. Until that day, enable me to lift Your name high in my community. Show me how to live so my actions and speech acknowledge You as Lord and point others to You. Help me honor Your name and always use it with respect and honor, giving You the place above all else in my life. Amen.

Nurturing

How precious to me are your thoughts, God!
How vast is the sum of them! Were I to count them,
they would outnumber the grains of sand—
when I awake, I am still with you.

PSALM 139:17–18

Praise God for His nurturing nature and care for you. Recall specific ways He has answered your prayers and met your needs, in ways both big and small.

Father, You are a good Father who knows what I need before I even ask (Matthew 6:8). You give good gifts to Your children, and I thank You for the many ways You have provided in my life. You care for me in ways I can't even imagine or understand. You know every detail of my life, down to the exact number of hairs on my head (Luke 12:7). You nurture and guide me in the way I should go, and even Your discipline is for my good and to help me grow (Hebrews 12:9). No one can measure Your thoughts. When I lie down to sleep, and when I wake in the morning, You are with me. You never leave or forsake me. I rest in Your care and trust Your nurturing provision for all my needs. Amen.

Overcoming Addictions

Because he himself suffered when he was tempted,
he is able to help those who are being tempted.

HEBREWS 2:18

———

Pray for those struggling with any type of addiction or self-medication that pulls their focus away from God's solution to pain. Pray for families affected by addiction. Pray against enabling or codependency. Ask God for complete healing of body, soul, and spirit.

———

Father, I confess it can be easy to fill life's voids with things other than You. I bring to You those struggling with addictions. Help all realize that willpower alone is not enough to bring deliverance from addiction's grip, but You are. May they see You as a God who understands our temptations and offers help. Bring a community who will speak the truth in love, who will give support, and who will do and say the hard things to bring help. Grant courage to do the hard work of recovery. May Your love be realized in fresh and new ways, and may the incredible value each life has to You be understood. Remove any shame, and may all experience the beautiful freedom that comes from releasing control to You. Give protection from those who would open the door back into the path of addiction. Through Your Holy Spirit, do a mighty, powerful healing work for Your glory. Amen.

Obedience to God

If you love me, keep my commands. . . .
Whoever has my commands and keeps them is the one
who loves me. The one who loves me will be loved by my Father,
and I too will love them and show myself to them.

JOHN 14:15, 21

Pray that you would be obedient to God in all areas of your life. Pray that your children or grandchildren will learn the blessings of obeying God early in their lives. Pray the churches in your community would be obedient to God's commands and through that obedience the light of Christ would shine.

Father, I love You and desire to keep Your commands. I want to be not just a hearer of the Word but someone who does what it says (James 1:22). Help me not to obey out of compulsion, out of obligation, or to keep up appearances, but out of my complete adoration of You. Bring my every thought and action under Your will. I pray my community would be so in love with You and Your words that obedience flows naturally out of our love for You. Give us strength to obey when it's hard and contrary to the world's way of living. Help us never to compromise or settle for anything less than complete obedience to Your Word. Give us understanding and show us how to live in obedience every day. Amen.

Ordinary Life

So whether you eat or drink or whatever you do,
do it all for the glory of God.

1 CORINTHIANS 10:31

Pray over the elements of your everyday, ordinary life. Remember to bring Him every detail—not just the big challenges, but also the daily routines—and seek to glorify Him in all you do.

Father, thank You for Your concern over every detail of life. Forgive me for the times when I've gone about my normal day and not given much thought to You or asked for Your direction. Today, as I go about my activities, I desire to honor You in everything. I bring these ordinary routines to You and invite You to be part of them. May my community not just come to You when we're in distress. Rather, help us recognize how much we need You every day, and how You desire to be part of every element of our community. Help us remember to open our hearts and lives to You and learn to recognize Your presence in the ordinary mundaneness of our everyday lives. Amen.

Omniscience

Great is our Lord and mighty in power;
his understanding has no limit.

Psalm 147:5

Praise God for His perfect knowledge of all things past, present, and future. Recognize that He is omniscient in your life and community, and that He sees what you do not. Praise Him that because He knows all, you have nothing to hide from Him.

Father, You are a great, all-knowing God. For all of eternity, You see and understand what was, what is, and what is yet to come. Your understanding has no limit, and I cannot comprehend Your might. You perfectly understand these situations that concern me and leave me wondering what the purpose is. Though I do not understand and only see such a small picture of what is happening, I trust You and Your knowledge to guide and provide. I praise You for working all things together for Your good (Romans 8:28). I praise You that because You already know all, I have nothing to hide from You. May my community be one that trusts in Your omniscient understanding. May we not rest and trust in our own limited knowledge, but always seek Your help and wisdom in all things. Amen.

Omnipresence

Where can I go from your Spirit?
Where can I flee from your presence?
If I go up to the heavens, you are there;
if I make my bed in the depths, you are there.
If I rise on the wings of the dawn,
if I settle on the far side of the sea,
even there your hand will guide me,
your right hand will hold me fast.

PSALM 139:7–10

Praise God for how He fills the universe with His presence and is present everywhere at once. Recognize how even when He seems distant in your life, He is still near to you.

Father, You are the ever-present, eternal God. There is nowhere I can go where You are not already there. From the deepest sea to the highest heaven, Your presence fills the space. Even when I cannot feel You, or Your voice seems silent, You are still close by. When I wandered away and had no thought of You, Your presence followed me. You fill even the darkest places. In the midst of the biggest battle and the most difficult heartache, You are present. Amen.

Pregnancies

For you created my inmost being;
you knit me together in my mother's womb.

PSALM 139:13

Pray for those who are pregnant. Pray for those who have unexpected pregnancies to have wise decision-making skills and support. Pray for those suffering from postpartum depression to receive help and experience hope and healing.

Father, You are the Creator of all life. You know us while we are still in our mothers' wombs, and You know all the days of our lives before they happen. Thank You for the lives growing within mothers. Protect the children growing inside them. May this be a special time of seeing You in deep and meaningful ways. Ease their fears and anxieties about giving birth. Should they experience complications in their pregnancies, help them know the peace and comfort of Your presence. Surround those with unexpected pregnancies with a community to love and support them long-term through the challenges ahead. For those who are suffering from depression and anxiety, give them courage to ask for help. Enable the community around them to see signs of their despair and offer help in ways they can accept. Help them to receive Your love and healing. Amen.

Persecution

Blessed are those who are persecuted because of righteousness,
for theirs is the kingdom of heaven. Blessed are you when people
insult you, persecute you and falsely say all kinds of evil against
you because of me. Rejoice and be glad, because great
is your reward in heaven, for in the same way
they persecuted the prophets who were before you.

MATTHEW 5:10–12

Pray for those who suffer persecution in your community, and for fellow believers across the globe. Pray for strength and sensitivity to the Holy Spirit, so when the day of persecution comes, followers of Christ can stand firm in their faith.

Father, You told us we would have trouble in this world, but to take comfort, for You have already overcome the world (John 16:33). Give strength and courage to all suffering persecution because of their faith in You. When they lose a job, are insulted, are falsely accused, or even have their lives threatened, help them respond in a way that shows a joy and a hope that only comes from You. Help us remember that we do not need to worry about we will do or say when the moment of persecution comes, for You have promised that the Holy Spirit will give us the words to say (Luke 12:11–12). Grow in us a sensitivity to Your Spirit so we can stand firm when trials come. Help us to remember our reward is in heaven and to rejoice in You no matter what happens. Amen.

Pain

He will wipe every tear from their eyes.
There will be no more death or mourning or crying or pain,
for the old order of things has passed away.

REVELATION 21:4

Pray for those in your community who live with continual physical pain. Pray for relief, the ability to cope, and protection from depression.

Father, I lift up individuals who struggle with physical pain on a daily basis. Pain interrupts their lives and prevents enjoyment of many activities they love. Help all in pain know they are not alone. Remind them to bring their pain to You, and provide the peace, comfort, and strength they need to get through each day. Enable each one to enjoy something they love today. Give doctors insight for how to manage the pain. Protect their mental health and keep them from slipping into the cavern of depression. Give patience and strength to their families and friends as they assist with activities their loved ones can no longer do. I boldly ask that You would heal them from their pain. Help us all look forward to the day when You wipe away every tear and there is no more pain. Until that day, we depend on You to get through each day. Amen.

Prince of Peace

For to us a child is born, to us a son is given,
and the government will be on his shoulders.
And he will be called Wonderful Counselor,
Mighty God, Everlasting Father, Prince of Peace.

Isaiah 9:6

Praise God and His Son, Jesus, as the Prince of Peace. Recall the ways He has brought His peace into your life and community.

Father, thank You for sending Your Son, Jesus, as the Prince of Peace. How our world desperately needs to know Your peace! I praise You for the ways You have brought Your peace into my life and community. You bring peace to disturbed relationships. You bring calm to my heart when I am anxious and afraid. Because of You, I can rest in Christ's love and know that sin no longer has power over me. I look forward to the day when Christ reigns as the Prince of Peace across the world and all creation lives in peace—even the wolf dwelling with the lamb (Isaiah 11:6). I praise You that because of Your righteousness, we can live in peace today, with the strength of quietness and confidence forever (Isaiah 32:17). You are the great Prince of Peace. Amen.

Promise Keeper

The Lord is not slow in keeping his promise,
as some understand slowness.
Instead he is patient with you, not wanting anyone
to perish, but everyone to come to repentance.

2 PETER 3:9

Praise God as the ultimate Promise Keeper, who sent His Son as our Redeemer. Recall the promises He has kept in your life and in your community.

Father, many people fail me, but You never fail. Your Word will endure forever (1 Peter 1:25). You always keep Your promises to Your people (Deuteronomy 7:9). You are patient, and through Your grace desire for all people to come to know You. I praise You for the promises You have kept in my life and community. You kept Your promise of a Redeemer through Jesus. You will keep Your promise of a home for eternity with You. Every need I have, You can meet. You've promised salvation, freedom, and that I can become a new creation. You've promised to teach me in the way I should go. You provided the promised Holy Spirit as my Helper. You've promised to always be with me and never leave me. I give praise that one day, Jesus will return on the clouds and set up His kingdom on earth, and will reign forever. I praise You for keeping all Your promises. Amen.

uniQue Needs

His disciples asked him, "Rabbi, who sinned,
this man or his parents, that he was born blind?"
"Neither this man nor his parents sinned," said Jesus,
"but this happened so that the works
of God might be displayed in him."

JOHN 9:2–3

Pray for families in your community with children who have unique needs, particularly special needs or challenging health situations. Pray for strength and endurance, protection for their marriages, wisdom for doctors, and an understanding community to surround them.

Father, please bring these families with unique needs an extra measure of Your love today. Show me how I can be a friend to them. Grant wisdom as they face challenging decisions about their child's health care. Give the doctors wisdom to direct their care. Bring special bonding among siblings and strengthen marriages during the extra stress of caring for their child. Show the churches in my community how to be welcoming places of respite, care, and company for these families. May they not feel isolated, but be surrounded with meaningful friendships to do life with. Amen.

Quandaries

I will instruct you and teach you in the way you should go;
I will counsel you with my loving eye on you.

PSALM 32:8

Bring your quandaries to God: all the things that perplex you and leave you uncertain about what to do. Pray over the difficult-to-solve dilemmas in your community. Thank God that He knows what you do not. Pray He will strengthen your faith when you do not see the answers.

Father, thank You for providing Your counsel and instruction in daily life. Please provide Your guidance in these situations where I am puzzled and not certain what to do. I give praise that my most perplexing problems are simple for You to solve. When I do not see the answer, strengthen my faith and help me grow. I thank You that You see what I do not, and I put my trust in You. Help me walk patiently by faith, not by sight (2 Corinthians 5:7). Teach me the way I should go. Counsel me, and remind me that Your loving eye is on me and I am not alone. My community has many situations that at times seem impossible to solve. Guide us to solutions that will honor You and bring glory to Your name. Help us take care of each other and love each other with Your love. I praise You, for no problem is too great or too small for Your care. Amen.

Qualms

Peace I leave with you; my peace I give you.
I do not give to you as the world gives.
Do not let your hearts be troubled and do not be afraid.

JOHN 14:27

Bring your qualms to God: your fears, the things that leave you uneasy, or situations you are apprehensive about. Pray over the fears of your community.

Father, the world is filled with things that often leave me uneasy, and afraid. In my daily life, I dread facing certain people and situations. When I wake up fearful of the day and what I must face, remind me that You walk with me. When the world feels overcome with hatred and evil, and I'm getting dragged into the current of despair, remind me that I do not need to be troubled or afraid. As a community, we are facing fears. Shine the light of Your peace into my community. As we go through these troubles, show us Your way of life. Help us follow the example of Jesus, who, when facing the darkest hour of His life, submitted Himself in to Your will. Amen.

Quieter of My Soul

The LORD your God in your midst,
The Mighty One, will save;
He will rejoice over you with gladness,
He will quiet you with His love,
He will rejoice over you with singing.
ZEPHANIAH 3:17 NKJV

Praise God as the Quieter of your soul. Recall the ways He has quieted you and your community during times of trouble.

Father, through all the qualms and quandaries of life, You are the Quieter of my soul. You are the Mighty One who saves me. I am humbled that You rejoice over me. I praise You for all the ways Your love has quieted me during times of trouble. Though the world around me seems to be falling apart, I have a quiet peace that comes only from You. When things stir in me a grief that nearly breaks my heart in two, You give a quiet confidence through Your Spirit (Isaiah 32:17). You are present in all my heartache. You lead me beside quiet waters, and You restore my soul (Psalm 23:2). I place all my hope and trust in You. Amen.

conQueror

And I looked, and behold, a white horse.
He who sat on it had a bow; and a crown was given to him,
and he went out conquering and to conquer.

REVELATION 6:2 NKJV

Praise God as the mighty Conqueror who will have the final and ultimate victory. Recall the ways He has conquered the enemy and defeated sin and death in your life and your community.

Father, You are the great Conqueror. Death has been swallowed up in victory, and it has no sting or power because You have defeated it (1 Corinthians 15:54–55). I give praise for how You have conquered the power of sin and death in my life. I am no longer a slave to the old life of sin. Your conquering power has given me freedom to live in victory through Your Holy Spirit. I give praise for how You have provided Your victory in my community. One day, Christ will provide the final victory over all the earth, and we will live in complete peace. Until that day, I praise You for the Holy Spirit, who gives life and freedom to all who believe in Christ. Amen.

Revival

Will you not revive us again,
that your people may rejoice in you?
PSALM 85:6

———————————

Pray for the Holy Spirit to move in people's hearts and bring renewed spiritual fervor. Pray that believers of Christ will have a passion for Him and His Word. Pray for pastors, teachers, and church leaders to stay true to God's Word in their teachings.

———————————

Father, I need Your Holy Spirit to move in people's hearts and bring a renewed spirit for You. Will You not revive us again? May a revival begin in my community, and may it begin in my heart. Reveal what is stealing our love and attention away from You, and remove any false gods from our lives. Shift us away from lukewarm faith, and light in us a passionate, all-consuming belief in You (Revelation 3:16). Awaken in us a deeper thirst and hunger for You and Your Word. Tear down the walls of our hearts. May we see Your truth, and may it set us free. Stir the pastors in my community into deeper devotion to You. Move through their faithful teaching of the Word to bring souls to dedicated faith in You. Have Your way in our hearts and lives, and launch a revival that stretches across our community and nation. Amen.

Raising Children

Let the little children come to me, and do not hinder them,
for the kingdom of God belongs to such as these.
Truly I tell you, anyone who will not receive
the kingdom of God like a little child will never enter it.

MARK 10:14–15

Pray for those who are raising children—whether their own children, grandchildren, or a friend or family member's children. Pray for each parent to have patience, perseverance, and love. Pray for wisdom in difficult situations, and for children to have hearts of obedience and honor.

Father, You created children, and You knew them before we did. You love them more than we can imagine. I bring these families raising children before You. You know the fears, insecurities, and challenges they each face. Give wisdom for difficult situations and the ability to raise their children in a way that points the children to You. May their discipline bring redemption. Grow in the children hearts of obedience and honor for You and their parents. May these families have a supportive faith and family community. When they are out of strength, patience, and hope, fill in the gaps. May they always remember that children are a gift from You. Amen.

Refugees

*The LORD is a refuge for the oppressed, a stronghold
in times of trouble. Those who know your name trust in you,
for you, LORD, have never forsaken those who seek you.*

PSALM 9:9–10

Pray for refugees in your community and for organizations
helping them settle into the community. Pray for those who
endured trauma or abuse, and for those who don't know the
language and culture. Pray for their home countries and family
members who might still be scattered or unsafe.

Father, You are a refuge for the oppressed, a stronghold in
times of trouble. Surround the refugees in my community
with Your love, friendship, and practical help as they transition
into their new lives. Thank You for a community willing
to offer a safe haven during their time of distress. Through
Your Spirit, bring healing from any abuse or trauma they have
suffered. Enable them to learn the language and culture and
ease the shock of transition. Give community leaders and local
organizations wisdom to know how to best meet their needs.
I pray for any missing family members who may be in unsafe
locations. Provide a way for them to connect with their families,
and bring a comforting peace while they wait for news
or safe arrival. I pray for peace for their home countries and
look forward to the day when Your peace will reign across the
world. Amen.

Redeemer

In him we have redemption through his blood,
the forgiveness of sins, in accordance
with the riches of God's grace that he lavished on us.

EPHESIANS 1:7–8

Praise God for sending His Son, Jesus, as the Redeemer who set you free from slavery to sin by His sacrifice on the cross. Praise Him for how He has revealed Himself to you, your family, and your community as the Redeemer. Praise God for redemption yet to come.

Father, You are the Almighty Redeemer. You have bought my salvation and freed me from the chains of sin and death through the sacrifice of Jesus Christ on the cross. Because of Your redeeming power, my old habits and ways of living no longer enslave me. All the wrong I have done or ever will do has been washed clean and forgiven through Christ's blood. It is a debt I can never repay, and I will never stop thanking You. I seek to praise You by making the most of every opportunity my new freedom affords and live a life worthy of this great price You have paid. I offer praise for the promise of the redemption yet to come—of creation itself and of our bodies (Romans 8:21, 23). I place my hope in You, my Redeemer. Amen.

Righteousness

My mouth will tell of your righteous deeds, of your saving acts
all day long—though I know not how to relate them all. . . .
Your righteousness, God, reaches to the heavens,
you who have done great things. Who is like you, God?

PSALM 71:15, 19

Praise God as the One who is righteous: completely right and just in all His ways. Praise Him for how He has given you His righteousness and restored your relationship with Himself.

Father, You are the only One who is completely right, just, and perfect in all Your ways. I am in awe that You, the perfect and holy God, desire a relationship with me. You provided the way for that relationship to be restored through Your Son. I give praise for Jesus, who knew no sin, yet became sin for me, so that His righteousness could be given to all who believe in Him (2 Corinthians 5:21). I do not have the words to proclaim the wonder of Your righteousness. It reaches to the stars, and nothing can ever compare to the majesty and power of Your righteousness. There is no one like You in the entire universe. You are the mighty Redeemer who has the power to save us. You are my righteous God. Amen.

*LORD, you alone are my portion and my cup;
you make my lot secure.*

PSALM 16:5

Pray for singles in all stages of life to have community, support, and purity, asking God to accomplish the fullness of His purpose in their lives. Pray for single parents to have support and encouragement, and that God would be their spouse and the fulfiller of all their needs.

Father, thank You for Your steadfast love for us in all situations. Today, grant the knowledge that You are with those who are single and that they are never alone. Help each one see in tangible ways how You are providing for every need. Provide friends who show Your love through acts of service, hugs, and kind words. Should they feel judged or like an outsider, remind them of the truth of who You say they are. Accomplish the fullness of Your purpose in each of their lives, and may all know the deep joy that comes from following You. Make Your presence known to single parents. When they are out of energy, give them the extra boost they need. Bring someone alongside them to offer encouragement and support. For those who desire marriage, grant them patience to wait and not rush into a relationship out of loneliness. Remind us all that our identity is not found in another person or relationship status, but in You. Amen.

Sexuality

Flee from sexual immorality. All other sins a person commits are outside the body, but whoever sins sexually, sins against their own body. Do you not know that your bodies are temples of the Holy Spirit, who is in you, whom you have received from God? You are not your own; you were bought at a price. Therefore honor God with your bodies.

1 Corinthians 6:18–20

Pray for sexual purity in your life, family, and community. Pray for protection against abuse, and healing for anyone traumatized by sexual abuse. Pray against the sexual exploitation of children, pornography, illicit sexual relationships, and the sex industry.

Father, help us see our sexuality in light of Your word. I pray for sexual purity in my life, and the lives of my family and children. Bring Your healing and love to all who suffer from sexual wounds and remove any shame. May Your light shine into the dark corners of our community, where sexual abuse and exploitation happens, especially to children. Provide hope and healing through the power of Your Spirit. Eradicate pornography from our homes, and guide us away from illicit sexual relationships. May the purity and beauty of Your design for sex within marriage be honored. Grant civic and spiritual organizations wisdom and strength to confront the sex industry in our community, and may the law enforcement and justice system convict the perpetrators. Amen.

Suicide

You have kept count of my tossings; put my tears in your bottle.
Are they not in your book? . . . For you have delivered
my soul from death, yes, my feet from falling,
that I may walk before God in the light of life.

PSALM 56:8, 13 ESV

Pray for those in your community with suicidal thoughts, that they will know their lives have value and they are loved. Pray that God will give hope, peace, and a sound mind and spirit. Pray for children and families in your community who have been affected by suicide, that they will know God's deep comfort.

Father, all life is precious and created by You. When I encounter someone who is silently struggling under the weight of hopelessness and believing that life has no value, may Your Spirit prompt me to offer words of hope and life. Help those contemplating suicide to accept love from You and others. Prompt people around them to show love and acceptance. Enable all to see the truth of their incredible value to You, to their families, and to friends. Defeat the lies they have believed or heard from others. Provide Your comforting hand to families whose loved ones took their own lives. Remove any guilt or shame they may feel, and bring a community to surround them with Your love long-term. Be with counselors and service providers helping them. When despair sets in, bring the hope and peace that comes only from You. Amen.

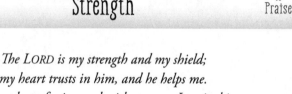

Strength

The LORD is my strength and my shield;
my heart trusts in him, and he helps me.
My heart leaps for joy, and with my song I praise him.
The LORD is the strength of his people,
a fortress of salvation for his anointed one.

PSALM 28:7–8

Praise God for His strength and for providing His strength to you as you face the struggles of life. Recall the ways He has been your strength in times past and present. Praise Him for how He provides His strength to your community.

Father, You are my strength and shield. I trust in You with all I have. I praise You for the ways You help me every day. Your strength has sustained me through the darkest days, through the rut of routine life, and it brings me boundless joy. Your strength defeats sin and delivers life where death once dominated. Your strength enables me to love as You love, even in the most difficult relationships. You are a strong tower, a safe place. I praise You for how You've given Your strength to our community during seasons of difficulty. You are the strength of my life. Amen.

Shepherd

The LORD is my shepherd, I lack nothing.
He makes me lie down in green pastures, he leads me beside
quiet waters, he refreshes my soul. He guides me along
the right paths for his name's sake. Even though I walk through
the darkest valley, I will fear no evil, for you are with me;
your rod and your staff, they comfort me.

PSALM 23:1–4

Praise God as the great Shepherd who leads you into quiet refreshment. Recall the ways He has been with you during the darkest valleys and given you His comfort. Praise Him for the ways He has guided you along the right path.

Father, You are the great Shepherd, who cares for His flock. You provide for my needs and give places of safety, rest, and refreshment. You gently lead and guide Your people. When I walk through the darkest times, even when I face death, I know I do not need to fear. You are with me, and You offer Your comfort and presence. I give praise for the ways You have refreshed and comforted me. I praise You for all the times when You have guided me along Your path. I trust You and praise You, the great Shepherd. Amen.

Teachers

In everything set them an example by doing what is good.
In your teaching show integrity, seriousness and soundness of
speech that cannot be condemned, so that those who oppose you
may be ashamed because they have nothing bad to say about us.

TITUS 2:7–8

———————

Pray for teachers of all grade levels, for patience, courage, wisdom, and love for their students and work. Pray against discouragement from the weight of external pressures, such as testing, standards, or lawmakers undermining the value of their work. Pray that their love and efforts working with children will be rewarded with many blessings.

———————

Father, please grant the teachers of my community wisdom, strength, knowledge, creativity, and a sense of humor. Help them see through the eyes of a child, and to see their students as You see them. Give them grace and patience for the challenges they face today, and may their attitudes remain positive and focused on the work You have for them. Enable them to build good relationships with their colleagues and administrators, so they may work together in the best interest of the students they serve. Encourage their hearts when they ache and struggle. Provide calm and grace when dealing with difficult parents and students. Refresh their love for their students today and give a renewed passion for their work. May they see Your love and faithfulness today. Amen.

Temptations

No temptation has overtaken you except what is common to mankind. And God is faithful; he will not let you be tempted beyond what you can bear. But when you are tempted, he will also provide a way out so that you can endure it.

1 Corinthians 10:13

———

Pray against temptations for yourself, your family, and your community. Bring God your struggles. Ask for His strength in the midst of the temptation and wisdom to see the way out.

———

Father, You are faithful and gracious, and I thank You for the help You provide when temptations come. I struggle desperately and need Your help with temptations. Help me resist and see the way out. Should I fail to refuse the temptation, prompt me to hear Your Spirit and return to You immediately and not walk in shame. Be with friends and family members in their struggles. When they face temptations, give them courage to walk away, strength to resist, and help for them to grow stronger and more like You as a result of the experience. Thank You for grace and forgiveness when we fall and for welcoming us back with open arms when we turn to You. Amen.

Trafficking

Speak up for those who cannot speak for themselves,
for the rights of all who are destitute. Speak up and judge fairly;
defend the rights of the poor and needy.

PROVERBS 31:8–9

Pray for those caught in human trafficking in your community. Ask God to shed light on this darkness, for community awareness, and for healing solutions. Pray that God will reveal Himself to each victim and protect their bodies, souls, and spirits. Pray for traffickers and clients to be caught and convicted, and that God would pierce their hearts and turn them to repentance.

Father, You set the captives free. Bring freedom to the people in my community held captive by human trafficking. Provide hope, and whisper to their spirits that they are not alone. Protect their bodies, souls, and spirits. Help my community hear their silent cries and have courage to speak on their behalf. Open our eyes and remove any denial that this happens in our community. Provide for the financial needs of the organizations helping and give them healing solutions. Bring conviction and justice to the perpetrators. Give the law enforcement and judicial system in my community the wisdom and skill to confront this issue and bring justice. Bring the purveyors of the industry into the light, and remove any legal loopholes so that they will be held accountable for their actions. Please eradicate this evil in my community. Amen.

Trustworthiness

Your kingdom is an everlasting kingdom,
and your dominion endures through all generations.
The LORD is trustworthy in all he promises
and faithful in all he does.

PSALM 145:13

Praise God for His trustworthiness. Recall how He has fulfilled His promises and been faithful, not just to you, but to your community and throughout all generations.

Father, You are trustworthy and steadfast. Your kingdom lasts through all generations. You keep Your promises and are always faithful. I praise You for showing me in Your Word how I can trust You. You delivered Your people from bondage and brought them into the Promised Land. Even though they were unfaithful, You kept Your promise to them. Through them You provided Jesus for all people, fulfilling the ultimate promise of redemption from sin. You are faithful in all You do. You've proven trustworthy in my life. I give praise for how You've displayed Your faithfulness in my community. Your trustworthiness will continue for all generations, and I desire to live my life in such a way that all around me can see how trustworthy You are. Amen.

Truth

If you hold to my teaching, you are really my disciples.
Then you will know the truth, and the truth will set you free.

John 8:31–32

Praise God that in a world of conflicting facts and opinions, He is Truth. Praise Him for how He made His truth known and set you and your community free through His Word, solid teachers, and His Holy Spirit.

Father, You are consistent, true, and unchanging in Your ways. In a world filled with confusing ideas and beliefs, I praise You for sending the Truth, Jesus, to show me the way to You (John 14:6). Thank You for how You've made Your truth known through Your Word and through Jesus. I praise You for helping me understand and live by the truth, and for how You've defeated lies in my life and set me free. I offer praise for how Your truth shines in my community through the churches and believers. Your truth is a light in the darkness, a path for my feet, and my hope for the future. Amen.

Unity

*Make every effort to keep the unity
of the Spirit through the bond of peace.*

EPHESIANS 4:3

Pray for unity among believers and for churches to come together in the name of Christ to love and serve the community. Pray for unity in families where there is division, and for relationships where there is strife. Pray for unity even among diversity and disagreement, for God's glory and honor.

Father, help me see where I can be a catalyst for unity in my community and spheres of influence. Show me Your compassion for the brokenhearted, and equip me with prayer, strength, and leadership to make an impact in the world for Your glory. Bring the churches in my community together in the name of Christ to serve the surrounding areas with love and practical help. Help Your Church to grow together in love seeking the common truth of Your grace. Enable unity in the most intimate places—our families. Help families in my community stand strong together in Your Word and in prayer. Where there are divisions, show how healing can begin, and let there be peace. Show us how the beauty of unity can thrive in the midst of diversity. Where our families, friendships, community groups, and churches experience disagreement, allow unity to continue for Your glory. Amen.

Unbelievers

This is how God showed his love among us:
He sent his one and only Son into the world
that we might live through him.
This is love: not that we loved God, but that he loved us
and sent his Son as an atoning sacrifice for our sins.

1 JOHN 4:9–10

Pray for the unbelievers in your community. Ask the Father to help them understand His love for them through Jesus. Pray that He might use you to reach them.

Father, Your love amazes me, and I can't thank You enough for how You've changed my life through Jesus. You desire for everyone to come to You with a repentant heart and accept Your salvation (2 Peter 3:9). By Your Spirit, soften hearts and prompt friends and family members to come to You. Abolish whatever prevents them from accepting You. May their hearts be open to Your love, and give them understanding of the great gift of salvation through Jesus. Help them see their need for You and how no sin is too great for Your forgiveness. Defeat the lies of the enemy occupying their minds, and open doors for me to speak the truth of Your love in ways they will hear and understand. Amen.

Ugly Thoughts

Finally, brothers and sisters, whatever is true, whatever is noble,
whatever is right, whatever is pure, whatever is lovely,
whatever is admirable—if anything is excellent
or praiseworthy—think about such things.

PHILIPPIANS 4:8

———————

Bring your inner life to God. Pray over any ugly thoughts no one else knows about. Ask for His help to create a clean and pure mind. Pray that God would be glorified in your heart and mind, praising Him for His forgiveness, grace, and mercy. Pray against any shame the enemy tries to put upon you, remembering God's truth instead of the enemy's lies.

———————

Father, You see who I am when no one else is around, and You know all my thoughts. Forgive me for where my thoughts have strayed from You and for when I've allowed hatred, jealousy, envy, selfishness, pettiness, and lust to occupy my mind. I desire to take every thought captive and make it obedient to You (2 Corinthians 10:5). Remind me how much my thoughts matter, and that as I think in my heart, so I am (Proverbs 23:7). Help me keep a pure mind, focusing on the true, noble, right, pure, lovely, admirable, excellent, and praiseworthy things, even when they are hard to find in the world around me. When my thoughts stray into sin, bring me to repentance and teach me to keep my mind steady on You. Amen.

Unchanging God

*Every good and perfect gift is from above,
coming down from the Father of the heavenly lights,
who does not change like shifting shadows.*

JAMES 1:17

Praise God for His unchanging nature, and how He is the same yesterday, today, and tomorrow. Praise Him for His unchanging love, holiness, and offer of forgiveness. Praise Him for being with you in the changing situations around you.

Father, You are the Giver of all good gifts, and I am overwhelmed by all You have given me. I am especially grateful for the knowledge of You and Your gift of salvation. You do not change (Malachi 3:6). You are the same today as You were yesterday and will be tomorrow too (Hebrews 13:8). I give praise for Your unchanging perfection and holiness and for Your enduring love for all people. I owe You all my praise for Your unmatched gift of forgiveness through Your Son, Jesus. Your Word does not change and will last forever (1 Peter 1:25). Your promises are sure. In the midst of these changing situations, I give praise, for You are with me and Your presence does not change. Amen.

Understanding

As a father has compassion on his children,
so the LORD has compassion on those who fear him;
for he knows how we are formed,
he remembers that we are dust.

PSALM 103:13–14

Praise God as an understanding Father who knows the weakness of your human flesh and has compassion on you. Praise Him for how He gives His understanding to those who follow Him and provides compassion for others. Praise Him for giving you His mind and heart to understand others when prejudices or judgments may blind you.

Father, You are a compassionate, understanding Father. I praise You for understanding my weaknesses and remembering the limitations of my earthly flesh. You are the Creator who made me, and You do not abandon Your children. Though I may fail to acknowledge and forget to follow You, You call me back to Yourself. I praise You, a Father who welcomes wandering children with open arms when they come home (Luke 15). You rejoice over each one who was lost but found. I praise You that when my prejudices and judgments cloud my perception, You give me Your heart and mind to understand others. Amen.

Violence

*For he will deliver the needy who cry out, the afflicted who have
no one to help. He will take pity on the weak and the needy
and save the needy from death. He will rescue them from
oppression and violence, for precious is their blood in his sight.*

PSALM 72:12–14

Pray against violence in your community. Pray for the hearts
of those causing violence to be reached with the truth of God's
love and their need for repentance. Pray for deliverance and
justice for those suffering from violence, whether in their
relationships or at the hands of strangers. Pray for children
who experience violence in their homes and don't know how
to ask for help, that God will give them courage and words to
request help.

Father, You love and rescue people from oppression and violence, and they are precious to You. We are desperate for Your
deliverance. I pray for all in my community who suffer from
acts of violence, behind closed doors, at the hands of people
they know and love, and especially for children who don't
know how to request help. Provide safe places and the words
they need to request help. Open my community's eyes and
ears to hear silent cries. Meet the needs of organizations, law
enforcement officials, and the judicial system as they enact justice. Call the hearts of those acting in violence to Yourself and
to repentance. Help our faith communities be safe places of
refuge for the hurting. Amen.

Vanity

Do nothing out of selfish ambition or vain conceit.
Rather, in humility value others above yourselves,
not looking to your own interests
but each of you to the interests of the others.
PHILIPPIANS 2:3–4

Pray against pride in your life and community—whether over appearances, abilities, or achievements. Confess any areas of vanity, and ask God to replace conceitedness with humility and a heart to serve others.

Father, I confess the areas of my life where I have been prideful over my appearances, talents, achievements, and abilities—all of which are gifts from You. Forgive me for exalting myself above others, even above You, and for not acting out of humility. Show me how to look out for the concerns and needs of others. Give me eyes and ears to see the needs around me and the ability to use my resources, talents, and abilities to serve others. Replace my pride with a humble heart of service toward You and the community around me. Help me not to seek praise and recognition from people. May my only desire be to hear from You, "Well done, good and faithful servant" (Matthew 25:21). May my community be known as one that is quick to humbly serve each other in Your name. Amen.

Vocation

As a prisoner for the Lord, then, I urge you to live a life
worthy of the calling you have received.
Be completely humble and gentle;
be patient, bearing with one another in love.

EPHESIANS 4:1–2

Pray over your vocational calling. Recognize that there is no separation between your life with God and your work life, but that all of your life belongs to Him. Pray for any tense work relationships and for strength to be like Christ in your responses to any friction.

Father, thank You for the gift of work. Thank You for opportunities to earn an income to meet my family's physical needs. Help me work with all my heart as though I am serving You, not a boss or a company (Colossians 3:23–24). I ask for the ability to extend grace in difficult work relationships. Help me be like Christ in my response to conflict. If I am asked to do something that goes against Your Word, grant me courage to speak up in a way that brings glory to You. Help me to love my coworkers as You do. In the areas where I need direction, please give me Your wisdom and guidance. May all I do and say during my working hours honor You. Amen.

Who is this coming from Edom, from Bozrah,
with his garments stained crimson? Who is this, robed in
splendor, striding forward in the greatness of his strength?
"It is I, proclaiming victory, mighty to save."

ISAIAH 63:1

Praise God for His victory over sin and death through Christ. Recall the ways He has brought His victory into your life and community. Offer praise for His victory, which overcomes the world and all the trouble in it.

Father, You are a victorious and mighty God. You have defeated Your enemy and delivered Your people from the restraints of sin and death. You have given all who follow Jesus Christ the victory, and sin holds no power over us (1 Corinthians 15:57). I offer praise for how You've delivered me from the grasp of sin and darkness through Jesus. I praise You for the victory You have given my community. Through You, we overcome the darkness in the world. Though the battle may feel all-consuming and wear us down, You renew our strength, and help us run and not grow weary, walk and not faint (Isaiah 40:31). Your victory overcomes the world (1 John 5:4). You are the victorious One, who is mighty to save. Amen.

Vine

I am the vine; you are the branches.
If you remain in me and I in you, you will bear much fruit;
apart from me you can do nothing.

JOHN 15:5

Praise God for the Vine, which is Christ, who grows His fruit in those who love and follow Him. Recall the things He has grown in your life. Offer praise for the good fruit you see in your community.

Father, I praise You for Jesus, the Vine that gives us eternal life. As I live my life connected to You, Your Spirit grows in me the miraculous fruit of love, joy, peace, patience, kindness, goodness, faithfulness, gentleness, and self-control (Galatians 5:22–23). Apart from You, I can do no good thing. My flesh is the way of death, but You give life everlasting. I praise You for not just demanding that we follow You, but providing the sustenance, knowledge, and strength to do so, as we stay connected to You through Your Word and through prayer. I praise You for the fruit of Your love growing in my community and through these people and churches. You are the Giver and Sustainer of life, the great Vine who feeds our souls. Amen.

Widows and Widowers

*Religion that God our Father accepts as pure and faultless is this:
to look after orphans and widows in their distress and to keep
oneself from being polluted by the world.*

JAMES 1:27

Pray for those who have lost their spouses to death and their families, for them to receive long-term support and provision for all their needs. Pray for their physical, emotional, and spiritual needs, and that God will be their Comforter in grief and loneliness.

Father, I bring these widows and widowers in my community to You. Bring peace and comfort in the midst of their overwhelming grief as only You can do. Give them enough strength and courage to face each day. Enable me to love them well. When the initial flood of calls and support has faded, continue to bring people to walk with them through the long, lonely season. Help them grieve well, but not remain in their grief forever. Provide grace to move forward day by day. May their hope rest in You and Your eternal love, and may they know You as their Sustainer, their Rock, their firm Foundation. Amen.

Wisdom

If any of you lacks wisdom, you should ask God,
who gives generously to all without finding fault,
and it will be given to you.

JAMES 1:5

Pray over the areas in which you and your community need wisdom. Pray for discernment in the ability to know, follow, and honor God in every area of life, especially during difficult times.

Father, thank You for generously offering Your wisdom to those who seek and follow You. Without Your wisdom, I have no insight into what is true or right in many situations. In these troublesome times, my heart's desire is to follow and honor You with my attitudes, actions, and decisions. Please show me the way of Your wisdom, which is always just and true. As I go about my day, may my mind and words be filled with the wisdom of Your Word. As a community, help us make wise decisions in caring for each other and providing help to those who need assistance. Please teach us and enable us to grow each day in Your wisdom. Amen.

Warfare

For our struggle is not against flesh and blood, but against the rulers, against the authorities, against the powers of this dark world and against the spiritual forces of evil in the heavenly realms. Therefore put on the full armor of God, so that when the day of evil comes, you may be able to stand your ground, and after you have done everything, to stand.

Ephesians 6:12–13

Pray for strength to stand firm in the midst of spiritual warfare in your life and community. Recall the ways He has helped you, your family, and community in the battle. Pray that God would give strength, equipping your community with the armor of God.

Father, thank You for giving us the tools to stand firm in the midst of spiritual battles. Help me remember that this fight isn't against other people, but against the powers of this dark world and the evil spiritual forces in the heavenly realms. Each day, empower me to stand firm surrounded with Your truth and living by righteousness. May my feet always be ready to move with the message of Your peace. Enable me to take up the shield of faith and combat the enemy's arrows sent against me. Guard my mind with the truth of Your salvation and remind me of the truth of Your Word, which is the greatest weapon. Help me stay alert and in prayer. Thank You for the ways You've helped me stand firm in the past and for how You are helping me now. Amen.

Worthiness

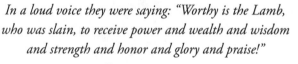
In a loud voice they were saying: "Worthy is the Lamb,
who was slain, to receive power and wealth and wisdom
and strength and honor and glory and praise!"

REVELATION 5:12

Praise God as the holy, almighty, worthy One. Proclaim, as the angels do, His worthiness of all your praise. Praise Him that because of His Son, you are worthy in His sight. Praise God that your worth is found in Jesus Christ, not in accomplishments or strengths, and that it is not diminished by weaknesses or failures.

Father, there is none like You. No other is as strong, righteous, or worthy to be praised as You. Through Your might and power You have defeated Your enemy and rescued Your people. You have unlimited power, are perfect in every way, and completely just. You created the earth and all that is in it. From the highest heaven, to the depths of the sea, You show Your power and creativity. Your beauty and magnificence shine brighter than the greatest star. You have done great works in my life and my community. I praise You that because of Your Son, I am worthy in Your sight. Thank You that my worthiness does not depend on my own goodness or strength and is not diminished by my failures. You are worthy of all the honor, fame, and worship I could ever offer. You are forever worthy to be praised. Amen.

Way

*Jesus answered, "I am the way and the truth and the life.
No one comes to the Father except through me."*

JOHN 14:6

Praise God for sending the Way, which is Jesus. Remember
how you first came to the Father through Jesus, and praise
God for opening the door to you. Praise Him for the people
and events He used to bring you to Himself.

Father, I praise You for creating a Way for me to come to You.
Through Your Son, Jesus, You opened the door for eternal life,
freedom from sin, and the ability to have a relationship with
You today. Without You, I would be lost, caught in a trap of
sin, and alone. I am humbled that You loved me enough to
make a way for me to come back to You, even before I knew I
needed You. You are the Way, the Truth, and my Life. Amen.

eXemplifying Christ

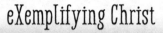

*Now this is eternal life: that they know you,
the only true God, and Jesus Christ, whom you have sent.*

JOHN 17:3

———————

Pray for opportunities to be the hands and feet of Christ and to share His message of love and forgiveness in your community.

———————

Father, I desire to see the name of Christ uplifted in my community. Jesus Christ is the Bread of Life, the Living Water, and my eternal hope. Give me courage to share this message of Your great love and salvation with my neighbors, friends, and family. Guide me by Your Spirit to make the most of every opportunity to share the knowledge of You with others. Help me speak the truth of Your salvation and forgiveness, and not be ashamed or afraid to speak up. Show me how I can share Your love through practical acts of kindness within my community. Help me recognize when Your Spirit is prompting me to send a message, share a smile, give a kind word, and meet a need. Help me not talk myself out of acting due to fear of what people might think. Instead, give me courage to move forward in faith. May all I do and say exemplify You. Amen.

eXamination

Search me, God, and know my heart;
test me and know my anxious thoughts.
See if there is any offensive way in me,
and lead me in the way everlasting.

PSALM 139:23–24

Spend time in prayer, asking God to examine every area of your life. Ask Him to reveal any sin, pride, or other places where you have been resisting Him. Confess your sins and ask Him to lead you into a life of obedience to His Word.

Father, I open up all of my life to You. Examine my heart, and show me where I am resisting You. Test my actions and reveal the times when I have acted out of pride and selfishness. I confess my sins and ask for Your forgiveness through Jesus Christ. Show me how to live in the way of Your Spirit and not my flesh. Help me to replace old, sinful habits with a new discipline of obedience to Your Word. Lead me in the way of freedom and eternal life. Convict my heart of the need for repentance when I stray. I love You and desire that nothing would get in the way of my relationship with You. Amen.

eXcessiveness

Then he said to them,
"Watch out! Be on your guard against all kinds of greed;
life does not consist in an abundance of possessions."

LUKE 12:15

Spend time praying over your material possessions and ask God to reveal any greed or idolatry. Pray against excessiveness and ask for strength to purge and let go of anything preventing you from serving Him wholeheartedly. Pray that your community would be free from excessive accumulation and be moved to generosity instead.

Father, it is easy to let possessions take precedence over You. Thank You for all the things I own; I recognize they are gifts from You. Help me use what I own and the income I make for Your glory and to further Your work. Reveal where I have been greedy. Prevent me from using material possessions to replace coming to You for safety, security, and significance. Show me where I have more than I need, and reveal how I can share my excess with those who could benefit from it. Help me not buy things I don't need, and grow in me a heart of generosity. May my community be one that willingly shares our resources with those in need. May we open our hearts and homes to You and each other, remembering that all we have comes from You. Amen.

eXcellence

Praise Him for His mighty acts;
Praise Him according to His excellent greatness!
PSALM 150:2 NKJV

Spend time praising God for the powerful things He has worked in your life and community. Praise His outstanding qualities and superiority in all He does.

Father, You are the most excellent in the entire universe. No one can describe all the mighty acts You have done. Were they to be written down, the paper would fill the whole earth. All You do is excellent, perfect, and just. Even when I do not understand Your ways, You are working the most excellent plan for Your glory and the good of those who love You (Romans 8:28). I praise You for the mighty things You have done in my life over the years. I praise You for the excellent work You are doing in my community. The most beautiful song ever written wouldn't be enough to describe Your greatness, for all You are and all You do is more wonderful than words can explain. You are the excellent Lord of all. Amen.

eXalting God

He says, "Be still, and know that I am God; I will be exalted among the nations, I will be exalted in the earth."

PSALM 46:10

Praise God for how He is exalted in the earth, how He's lifted high in your community, and His elevated nature above all creation. Recall the ways you see Him exalted in your life, in nature around you, and in relationships in your community.

Father, there is no one higher than You. No one is greater or more powerful than You in all the earth. Your power shines through creation, and You work wonders of forgiveness and restoration in my life. I praise and exalt You for the ways I have seen Your power rise above troubles and trials in my life. I praise You for how You have been lifted up in my community. You are worthy of all honor and glory. When darkness seems to rule, You are still at work and will be exalted above all else. You are the victorious King who comes in power and will reign forever. Be exalted in my life and community. Amen.

Don't let anyone look down on you because you are young,
but set an example for the believers in speech,
in conduct, in love, in faith and in purity.

1 Timothy 4:12

Pray for children, teens, and young adults in your community, for their spiritual growth and purity, and that they may grow into adults who love and serve God. Pray that they will be leaders in their generation and will find their worth and purpose in God, not in the values of the world. Pray protection over their hearts and that they will share their love for Jesus with their peers who don't know Him.

Father, help me walk alongside the youth in my community. I ask especially for them to know You in a deep and personal way. May I and other followers of You be mentors and guides who will point them to You. Whether it's taking them to church with us, relating our stories, or just being a friend, help us share Your love and words of truth with them. Raise up a generation of youth who will passionately follow You their whole lives. Be with the youth leaders, pastors, mentors, and parents who are guiding them. Protect them from rebellion or activities that give the enemy a foothold. Guard them and the plans You have for their lives. Amen.

Yearnings

My soul yearns, even faints, for the courts of the LORD;
my heart and my flesh cry out for the living God.

PSALM 84:2

Give your yearnings to God—your strong desires and longings in life that have gone unfulfilled. Give Him the yearnings for your community, and ask Him to fulfill your desires with Himself and His will.

Father, my heart holds many unfulfilled longings. I lay these yearnings at Your feet and trust that Your will for my life is better than anything I could ask or imagine on my own (Ephesians 3:20). I commit the desires of my heart to You and seek to make my delight in You—not in the hope of what may come (Psalm 37:4). Help me abandon any sinful yearnings, and grow in me a life that pursues righteousness, faith, love, and peace (2 Timothy 2:22). May Your will be done in my community, and fill us with the light of Your presence. Make our yearning, our greatest desire, be for You. Amen.

Yielding

Do not go on offering members of your body to sin as instruments
of wickedness. But offer yourselves to God [in a decisive act]
as those alive [raised] from the dead [to a new life], and your
members [all of your abilities—sanctified, set apart]
as instruments of righteousness [yielded] to God.

ROMANS 6:13 AMP

Yield all of yourself—your desires, body, and talents—to God. Surrender control and give the power and authority over your life, family, and community to Him. Pray that God will work His will in your life through the power of His Holy Spirit living inside you.

Father, I offer all I am to You. It's easy to think that I am in control of my life and that I can go and do as I please. I surrender control over my life, family, and community to You. Do Your work in me through Your Holy Spirit, and make my life a pleasing offering to You. I relinquish all power and authority to You. May my body, mind, skills, vocation, and hobbies be instruments for sharing Your love with others. Forgive me for where I have taken control and made a mess of things because of my sin and selfishness. Amen.

Yahweh

God said to Moses, "I AM WHO I AM.
This is what you are to say to the Israelites:
'I AM has sent me to you.'"

EXODUS 3:14

Praise God as Yahweh—the great I AM—the name He revealed to His people. Praise Him as the God who always was and always will be.

Father, many things in life come and go, yet You remain. You are the great I AM who revealed Himself to His people. You do not change (Malachi 3:6). You are the eternal God who makes Himself known to us through Jesus, who proclaimed, "Before Abraham was born, I am!" (John 8:58). You reveal Yourself through Your Word, through creation, and now through Your Holy Spirit. When I am lacking courage and fearful of the world around me, You are present. You are the eternal God, the Almighty, the Holy One. You were before the world was formed, and You always will be. My finite mind cannot comprehend You, and seeing just a glimpse of You fills my heart with awe. You do not share Your glory with any other being. You are the one, the only, the great I AM, forever and ever. Amen.

Yoke

*Take my yoke upon you and learn from me, for I am gentle
and humble in heart, and you will find rest for your souls.
For my yoke is easy and my burden is light.*

Matthew 11:29–30

―――――――

Praise God that when you join your life with His, He gently
teaches and leads you in the way you should go. Offer praise
for how, in this joined-together life, you have experienced
His rest.

―――――――

Father, You are a mighty God, yet One who is gentle and
humble in heart when engaging Your people. I praise You for
the gift of joining my life with Yours. As I submit my life to
serve You, You teach me right living. Thank You for the ease
of Your yoke. Although this right life is not "easy," when I am
submitted to You, I have peace and contentment I cannot find
anywhere else. I praise You for the rest You've brought into my
life. When I come to You, I am able to stop working for my
salvation or trying to be good enough to earn Your approval.
Instead, You gently remind me how the work has already been
done through Christ, and You refresh me from my wearying
activities. I cannot praise You enough for the gift of this yoked
together life. Amen.

Zero Prejudice

There is neither Jew nor Gentile, neither slave nor free,
nor is there male and female,
for you are all one in Christ Jesus.

GALATIANS 3:28

Pray for healing of racial tensions in your community and for the elimination of all types of prejudices. Pray that you would see each person as a valued image-bearer of God. Pray for love across all races, religions, and genders, while not compromising the truth of God's Word.

Father, the world today is ripped open with bitter conflict, racial tensions, and religious and gender prejudices. Convict me, Lord, where I have prejudice and stereotypes, and through Your Holy Spirit replace these things with honor and love for others. Help me see people who are different from me through Your eyes. Bring healing from racial tensions and religious and gender prejudices in my community. I ask for Your help to love my neighbors as myself and realize that everyone is valuable to You. Give us all courage to speak and act in someone's defense when we see an injustice happen, whether in a prejudiced word or action. Help us share Your love with those around us and break down the barriers of prejudice in our communities. Amen.

Zodiac

He determines the number of the stars
and calls them each by name.

PSALM 147:4

Pray for those in your community who look to astrology and the stars for understanding, direction, and hope for their lives. Pray the stars instead would awaken a wonder for the God who created the stars and that they might see His faithfulness in their lives.

Father, You have stretched out the heavens (Zechariah 12:1). You placed the stars in the sky and call each one by name. The stars, sun, and moon not only light our days and nights and mark the seasons, but they display Your majesty and power. I pray for those in my community who look to the stars for guidance and understanding and don't know You as the One who will guide them if they only seek You. I ask that, as they study the zodiac and read the signs, the light of the stars would reveal the knowledge and hope of You. May they search beyond the sky for answers and find You in Your Word and through the people around them. Help all see Your guidance and faithfulness in their lives. Stir a longing that can be satisfied only by You. Light the way to Yourself. Amen.

Zest

You make known to me the path of life;
you will fill me with joy in your presence,
with eternal pleasures at your right hand.

PSALM 16:11

Pray that God will fill you with zest—a hearty enjoyment and passion—for Him and for the life He has given you. Ask Him to fill your community and area churches with deep enjoyment of His presence.

Father, You have shown the way to true and eternal life. You light a path through this dark world and offer joy that I did not realize was possible, even during the deepest pain. Please fill me with an enduring zest for You. Help me to remember that following You isn't a list of rules to keep, but an opportunity to enjoy You and the gifts You offer. Fill me with passion for You, and may my service to You flow out of a deep love and loyalty to You, not a drudgery of duty and obligation. Fill the churches in my community with Your presence. May they experience zest while worshiping in Your presence and serving each other throughout the week. May we seek to enjoy You and Your presence each day we live on this earth. Amen.

But you have come to Mount Zion, to the city of the living God,
the heavenly Jerusalem. You have come to thousands
upon thousands of angels in joyful assembly.

Hebrews 12:22

Praise God as the ruler of Zion and for the promised home we have with Him for eternity.

Father, You are the great Ruler of all eternity. You have established Mount Zion, Your city, which has no end. You live in the presence of angels who offer ceaseless praise in a place of deep joy and worship. No place on earth or any beauty of creation could ever compare to the glory and wonder of Zion. The Psalmist said that those who trust in You would be like Mount Zion, not shaken and enduring forever (Psalm 125:1). I praise You for how You have kept me firm when I felt like everything was falling apart. Thank You for the future promised home in Your city for all who follow You (John 14:3). I look forward to the day when You will return and take Your children home to be with You in Zion forever. Amen.

Zeal

*Of the greatness of his government and peace there
will be no end. He will reign on David's throne and over
his kingdom, establishing and upholding it with justice
and righteousness from that time on and forever.
The zeal of the LORD Almighty will accomplish this.*

Isaiah 9:7

––––––––––––––

Praise God for His intense passion and diligence toward His people and His name, which will result in the eternal reign of Christ over the earth. Recall how you have seen His zeal accomplishing great works in Scripture, your life, and your community.

––––––––––––––

Father, I cannot comprehend how great You are. Your intense passion for Your people and Your name will result in the greatest rule ever on earth. You will right every wrong and uphold justice and righteousness for eternity. I give praise for how You will keep Your promise to return and set up Your kingdom here on earth. Your zeal for my life astounds and humbles me. I praise You for how Your loving patience and passion has moved and changed my life. You have worked great things in my community. Your diligence to us cannot be matched. You are a zealous God who never fails His people. Amen.

Acknowledgments

To Kedron: This book would never have happened without your love and support. From the moment I showed you the initial A to Z list, you believed God had a special plan for this. Thank you for lending your design skills, pouring belief into me, and in general keeping our household together. ILY.

To Ilana and Titus: You are the greatest kids a mom could ever ask for. Thanks for all your help and always reminding me that it will work out okay. Love you bunches.

To my parents, Steven and Joyce, and my in-laws, Sheldon and Victoria: Thank you for your love and prayers. I couldn't have asked for better parents and grandparents for my kids. I wouldn't have met my deadline were it not for all the times you took care of the kids. They love hanging out with you. Bless you.

To the community of friends who willingly shared their stories on my blog in the original Pray A to Z series—Cindy J., Brenda Y., Martie B., Susie F., Tanya G., Nicole H., Amy S., Carrie V., Gary W., Tim P., Paul and Edith C., Cindy B., Jen F., Lisa L., Ellen S., Jason H., Sharron C., Becky D., Lisa V., Colleen R. M., Andrew R., Dan S., Jenna S., and Bobby V.: Your stories touched many and taught us how to love and pray for the people around us. Thank you.

To the Florida friends who've shared so much life with my family—the Hudsons and Vargheses: Our love reaches across the miles each day. You'll always be an important part of our community.

To my writers group—Brenda, Elizabeth, Jane, Bonnie, and Robin: Thank you for encouraging and praying me through the writing process and reading early drafts. I'm thankful for each of you and so happy God brought our group together.

To my Breathe Christian Writers Conference planning committee friends—Ann, Sharron, Denise, Susie, Alexis, Cassie, and Darron: It's a privilege to serve with you. Your encouragement for this project from the beginning has kept me going.

To the long list of friends and family who faithfully prayed through the writing of this book: You are a gift, and I'm so thankful for your partnership in this good work. Michelle, Carlie, Karon, and Shayna, you're the greatest group of sisters-in-law a gal could ever ask for. Thanks for sharing this with your friends, praying big for it, and being my travel buddies at events. Kristi, thanks for all the long runs and listening to me talk for miles. Susie, thanks for checking in on me, praying, and talking me back to reality.

To the town of Lowell: You provide a great example of a community that stands together and supports each other through the fiercest of storms. I love living here. Thank you for welcoming my family.

To my agent, Wendy Lawton, and the team at Books & Such Literary Agency: Thank you for your support and encouragement over the years. Wendy, thank you for taking my stack of cards and seeing the potential for what God might have in store.

To Pamela Clements and the team at Worthy Inspired: Thank you for believing in this project and pouring your gifts into serving God through it. I'm honored to work with such a dedicated and skilled team.

To my heavenly Father: Without You, my life would be a complete disaster. I owe You everything and humbly offer these words to You. Because of Your Son, Jesus, we can come boldly to Your throne.

Amelia Rhodes lives in Lowell, Michigan, with her husband and two children. As a recovering perfectionist who has been freed, by God's grace, from the grip of perpetual anxiety, Amelia encourages women to discover who they are in Christ and to deepen their relationships with each other. Her favorite activities include coffee breaks and pizza parties with friends and family.

Amelia has written for *The Upper Room* devotional, GEMS Girls' Clubs, and four *Chicken Soup for the Soul* books. Her first book, *Isn't It Time for a Coffee Break?*, encourages women to deepen their friendships.

You can connect with Amelia online at:

www.ameliarhodes.com

 facebook.com/ameliarhodeswriter

 @amrhodes

 @ameliamrhodes